7 Course Meal
for the
SOUL

Human Consciousness Technology 7.0

An easy-to-read overview of the World's Greatest
Teachings on Ultimate Happiness

ANGI COVINGTON

BALBOA.
PRESS
A DIVISION OF HAY HOUSE

Balboa Press books may be ordered through booksellers or by contacting:
Balboa Press
A Division of Hay House
1663 Liberty Drive
Bloomington, IN 47403
www.balboapress.com
1-(877) 407-4847

Printed in the United States of America.

ISBN: 978-1-4525-7729-6 (sc)
ISBN: 978-1-4525-7731-9 (hc)
ISBN: 978-1-4525-7730-2 (e)

Library of Congress Control Number: 2013913977

Balboa Press rev. date: 11/4/2013

Table of Contents

Part 1 - Our Purpose

Part 2 - The Menu

Part 3 - Experiencing the Meal

Foreword

I first met Angi Covington in March of 2008, when my wife asked me to attend a class with her called "7 Course Meal for the Soul" at a local women's center.

During the two hour session, Ms. Covington covered seven things that promised to lead us to a place of Ultimate Happiness. While the teachings made sense, there was one thing that really impressed me. The way I felt at the end of the session.

When we first arrived for the class I was a little frustrated with having to be there at all, but I reminded myself I was really there to support my wife's interest in the topic. By the end of the session I felt much more calm and relaxed. Considering the work I do and the general level of stress I have daily, this calmness was a welcome change from my normal state. Given Angi's corporate background and professional presentation style, I invited her to present the program to my Executive Team at our next staff meeting. To be frank, I thought some members of my team might think she was a little crazy and that I was crazy for inviting her to present a program for the soul. After all, we are speaking about a team of prison professionals, many with over 25 years in the field. To my surprise, all the comments were positive. At a minimum, all appreciated the opportunity to take a few minutes to slow down from their otherwise stressful day.

During our debrief meeting, Angi mentioned that she had an interest in working with inmates. With buy in from the Wardens, she began teaching the "7 Course Meal for the Soul" program over a seven week period to both female and male inmate populations.

During my 45 years in corrections, we only randomly impacted recidivism. When I began my service as Director with the Nevada Department of Corrections, I thought my legacy was going to be quite different. But with budgets what they were, I am beginning to wonder if my legacy may be making programs of this kind available to the inmate population. Again, while we have no hard data regarding this program and recidivism, I've seen enough to believe it's worthy of consideration.

I am grateful for Angi's commitment to our Southern Nevada inmates. She did all of her teaching on a volunteer basis, and personally bought a book for every inmate who's graduated from the class.

I would like to personally thank you for purchasing this book, as it allows Ms. Covington to continue her impactful work.

If Ms. Covington can help men and women find happiness in prison, I am confident she can help you and your organization, do the same.

Howard Skolnik
Former Director, Nevada Department of Corrections

Part 1

Our Purpose

One Wish

Today may seem like any other day. You've gone about your regular routine working, playing, stressing, relaxing, worrying, dreaming, thinking, feeling, taking care of everyone else—you know the drill. However, I believe today will prove to be very different.

What you'll read in this book is not only for the mind to understand, it will also serve as nourishment for the soul.

Since the soul likes to have fun and play, let's start off with a game my friends and I used to play as children.

> *"It is a happy talent to know how to play."*
> *-Ralph Waldo Emerson (1803-1882)*
> *American Philosopher & Poet*

It's called "One Wish". Here's how it works: you get one wish for anything you want. But there is one limitation, you can't wish for more wishes. Other than that, the sky's the limit. Go ahead and take a minute to think about it. Choose carefully, because you only get one.

Once you've decided, please pause here and note what you'd wish for.

_____

_____

_____

_____

_____

So, what did you wish for?

Success? Money? Millions? Billions? A mansion? Your dream car? A luxury vacation? The opportunity to travel around the world? A new wardrobe? Something to make your family's life easier? Maybe you wished for some change to your physical appearance. Maybe you just want everyone to think you're hot!

Maybe you think material things are superficial. Did you wish for that special someone, your soul mate? Someone who will love and accept you exactly as you are? Maybe you wished for good health or eternal health for someone you love. Did you wish for a child? Maybe you just want to be respected or revered by others.

Or are you more spiritual? Did you wish for enlightenment? Maybe you want to experience some of the inexplicable magic the universe holds. How about an out-of-body experience? Maybe you wished to be free of the ego altogether. Would you like to read minds? Maybe you want to be the best version of you that you can possibly be.

Maybe you have desires that go beyond you. Did you wish for world peace? Maybe you wished to leave your mark. You know, change the world for the better. Did you wish to save man from himself?

You may have wished for something I haven't even mentioned.

Whatever you wished for, take a moment to think about why you would use your one and only wish on that.

Deep down inside, why do you want that one thing above all others? What will it give you?

_____

_____

_____

_____

When you get down to the very core of it, I'll bet you wished that wish because you think it will make you happy.

That's the one wish we all have in common. While we may have different ideas about what it is that will make us happy, every human being is *hungry* to be happy. Background doesn't matter.

Education, status, age, looks, achievements, experience—none of these things matter. We all just want to be happy. Being happy will make us feel *full*. Doesn't seem like a tall order does it? Yet here we are in the twenty-first century, and this is the one thing that still seems to elude mankind.

We have made amazing advancements in so many areas. Technology allows us to accomplish feats that are Jetson-like. Our cars can give us directions. The internet gives us instant access to answers for any question we may have, wirelessly. Advancements in biotechnology have many experts predicting we'll be able to buy an artificial version of any body part, except the brain and central nervous system, by the 2020's. We have more entertainment options than ever. We have billions of *things*, all designed to make our lives easier—to make us happy.

Despite all our achievements, why are there so many people who are still unhappy? We seem to be starving for happiness. It seems the more things, choices, achievements and opportunities, we have, the hungrier we've become.

Please consider the following information that demonstrates the impact of our nation's stress and unhappiness:

A June, 2012, article published by the American Psychological Association stated:

- The use of psychotropic drugs by adult Americans increased 22 percent from 2001 to 2010, with one in five adults now taking at least one psychotropic medication
- In 2010, Americans spent more than $16 billion on antipsychotics, $11 billion on antidepressants and $7 billion for drugs to treat attention-deficit hyperactivity disorder

According to a 2011 study in the PloS ONE journal:
- Tweets steadily trended towards unhappiness over a three year period.

From Gallup's 2013 State of the Workplace Report:
- The vast majority of U.S. workers are actively disengaged and not reaching their full potential—a problem that has significant implications for the economy and the individual performance of American companies.

- Gallup estimates that active disengagement costs the U.S. $450 billion to $550 billion per year

To put this in perspective, $550 billion is sixty-seven percent of the net profits from **all** Fortune 500 companies combined.

Another APA article called "How Does Stress Affect Us?" reports:
- 75 to 90 percent of all physician office visits are for stress-related ailments and complaints.

Stress is linked to the six leading causes of death—heart disease, cancer, lung ailments, accidents, cirrhosis of the liver, and suicide.

In a 2010 blog, Robert Leahy, Ph.D., Director, American Institute for Cognitive Therapy in New York City wrote:
- Depression is widespread and it is getting worse.
- Sadly, it hits the young and old alike.
- Depression has human costs that we all know of: sadness, sense of isolation, feeling like a burden, inability to enjoy life and suicide. There are also economic costs that are also significant—indeed, alarming.
- Depressed individuals are five times more likely to abuse drugs.
- Depression is the leading cause of medical disability for people aged 14 to 44.
- People with symptoms of depression are 2.17 times more likely to take sick days. And when they are at work their productivity is impaired—less ability to concentrate, lower efficiency, and less ability to organize work.
- In one study the costs of absenteeism were directly related to actually taking antidepressant medication.

I did not include numbers related to addiction—injuries, health implications, productivity loss or workplace violence (which is on the rise). But I'm sure I've made the point: unhappiness is costing us a fortune!

Considering these costs, it sounds like starvation to me. And the problem is not limited to the United States. Back in 1992, a United Nations report labeled stress "The 20th Century Disease" and a few years later the World Health Organization said it had become a "World Wide Epidemic."

What could we accomplish with improved health and vitality that may come from happiness and reduced stress? How might we relate with the rest of the world if we were happier? What good could we do with those hundreds of billions of dollars we'd be saving?

Less staggering, yet still impactful, let's take a look at the costs on an individual level. What is the lack of ultimate happiness costing you? Please pause for a moment to really answer that question. What is unhappiness costing you? Where do you spend money or time, in pursuit of happiness? Do you have addictions? How is unhappiness affecting your relationships? Your energy? Your health? Your outlook on life? Your future?

_____

_____

_____

_____

_____

_____

_____

This is why our paths have crossed. I am here to share a meal that will *nourish* you. It will give your life the *full* feeling that only ultimate happiness can give. I am here to serve as your maître d' and my goal is to translate the menu for you—a menu consisting of seven courses that will nourish the soul.

This meal has been prepared for you over thousands of years by some of the world's greatest chefs (leaders, teachers, philosophers, gurus, scientists, inventors and masters).

Please join me, as I take you to your table.

"When one reaches happiness, one is close to perfection."
-Chuang Tzu (396 BC-286 BC)
Taoist Sage

Your Maître d'

Allow me to formally welcome you to our restaurant. My name is Angi Covington and I will serve as your maître d'. My goal is to help you navigate the menu in a way that is clear and simple. Before we begin, I think it's important that I share a little about my background and how I came to this restaurant.

Background

I have considered myself a student of human behavior for almost forty years. I love observing people and understanding how we operate; why we "do what we do" has always intrigued me.

As a teenager I had some unique views about the world and didn't have much interest in the traditional educational system. I always tested high on aptitude tests but found myself bored and unstimulated. After dropping out of high school twice, I discovered that I might be able to make an income doing something I was interested in. What else would interest a teenage girl besides boys or her friends? Clothes! So, I finished two and a half years of coursework in about six months, through an alternative high school we called "Drop-In". I went on to receive an associate degree from a fashion & art institute and a bachelor's degree in marketing. I'd begun working on a master's degree when I decided what I really wanted was a degree in life.

My continuing interest in people led me to a career that has hovered in three areas; sales, corporate training and management. I would estimate that the companies I have worked for have invested approximately $500,000 to formally educate me in the area of human behavior. This education has given me a pretty good understanding of how human beings operate and what drives us.

I created a life for myself that made me pretty happy. I spent thirteen years in the wireless technology industry. I received several promotions and awards, made a good income, bought a nice house, drove various luxury cars and built a decent retirement account. Then a new four letter word entered my life: merger. Yes, I know it's not really four letters, but maybe it should be. Let's just say the new company's culture did not make me feel very happy. So, I resigned my position, cashed in my stock options and went in search of what I would do with the next chapter of my life.

I took a two and a half year sabbatical, setting out to find the key to ultimate happiness. I took classes and read books on topics ranging from the brain to spirituality. I attended self-improvement courses, practiced Buddhism for a time and studied under masters around the world. I've been to India three times and was a student at a spiritual university there. During one visit I spent seventeen days in complete silence, which included having no eye contact with anyone. This was an amazing accomplishment, as I have always been a talker. In first grade my teacher wrote, "Talks too much," on my report card.

I found myself intrigued by how many people were searching for ultimate happiness. After personally investing another $50,000, I think I finally got it.

Why Write this Book

Trust me when I tell you, the last thing this world needs is another book or seminar on "How to Be Happy". I attended seminars and read what seems like hundreds of books and I'm certain I didn't make a dent in what's out there. Each promised to hold the key. Knowing this, why would I consider writing yet another one? I fought it for a long time, but two reasons kept coming back to me.

First, I couldn't stop thinking about all those billions we are spending on our unhappiness. I think about how that money could affect our economy, our educational system and our nation's future.

Don't get me wrong, I like feeling happy and I enjoy being around happy people. But I still think like a business person and the numbers speak volumes. Not only is unhappiness costing us through our spending, we are also missing the potential revenues that would come from being happy.

- Happy employees = cost reductions (billions in healthcare and drug related expenses alone) = **increased net profits**
- Happy employees are more loyal = reduced turnover = **increased net profits**
- Happy employees produce more = **increased net profits**
- Happy employees miss fewer days of work = increased production by executives and employees who are actually at work = **increased net profits**
- Happy employees produce a better quality output = reduced QC costs + increased customer loyalty + referrals/increased sales = **increased net profits**
- Happy employees provide better customer service = customer loyalty + referrals/increased sales = increased revenues = **increased net profits**
- Happy employees are contagious = **we all get to be happy!**

Can you say increased net profits? It's not hard to do the math; happiness can be very profitable. And we all get to be happier?! This is what I'd call a WIN-WIN!

"The evidence is clear: People perform better when they're happier."
-Dr. Teresa Amabile (born 1949 or 1950)
Edsel Bryant Ford Professor of Business Administration
and a Director of Research, Harvard Business School

However, I don't know anyone in the corporate world who has a spare week on their calendar, let alone a month or a year to go on an expedition for ultimate happiness. And how many people in this country have thousands of dollars to spare, to invest in this quest?

This leads to the other reason I chose to write this book, my skill set. I honed two skills while working in the wireless industry:

1. Sift through large amounts of information and pull out the highlights for executives or clients, who don't have a lot of time.
2. Take complex information and present it in a way that can be easily understood by anyone.

*"I have deep faith that the principle
of the universe will be beautiful and simple."*
-Albert Einstein (1879-1955)
Physicist & Philosopher, Nobel Prize in Physics (1921)

I believe this topic could benefit from both of these skills:

1. As mentioned, I've sifted through plenty of information on finding ultimate happiness, discovered the common threads in the teachings and I am prepared to deliver the following (choose the one that fits your preferred terminology):
    *   Executive Dashboard
    *   Easy to Read Overview
    *   50,000 ft. View
    *   Concise presentation of the commonalties in the world's greatest teachings on the subject
2. Talk about complex—I have a pretty decent IQ, but I had to re-read some of the teachings multiple times to make sense of them. Now that I've developed a pretty good understanding, I can share the highlights of the teachings in a way that can easily be understood by anyone.

"Genius is the ability to reduce the complicated to the simple."
-C.W. Ceram (1915-1972)
German Journalist & Author known for his works about Archaeology

As your maître d', I am here to save you time and money, while still helping you to get the outcome we are all looking for—ultimate happiness.

About the Meal

There are a few things that will be helpful for you to understand before we get into the menu.

Digestion Advisory

- It is my hope that you will be able to enjoy the meal for what it is—a means to satiate our hunger for ultimate happiness.
- If you are a spiritual seeker, consuming this meal may cause indigestion. Its simplicity may cause slight discomfort and bloating.
- This meal has been designed for people who haven't the time, money or desire to do the work of a seeker.
- If you are hungry for mystical or metaphysical experiences such as out-of-body experiences, seeing angels or experiencing other dimensions, please be advised this restaurant doesn't serve those menu items.
- During this meal, I'll be sharing quotes from various chefs (teachers) which support the menu items. There will also be references to the Head Chef (God, Buddha, Allah, Yahweh, Universal Energy, et al.) but this meal is not about taking sides for what you believe. It is intended for all palates (beliefs or faiths).

"You're basically killing each other
to see who's got the better imaginary friend."
-Yasser Arafat (1929-2004)
Palestinian Leader, Nobel Peace Prize (1994)

My goal is to show you that the teachings all say virtually the same things. So, if you are Christian, Buddhist, Muslim, Hindu, spiritual but not religious or atheist, I honor your beliefs. I will attempt to show you the similarities, no matter what you believe.

Origin of the Meal

This meal has been created from ingredients (teachings) that have been around for thousands of years. They are from both ancient and modern day teachers. As your maître d', I did not create the menu. I didn't even enter the kitchen.

I do however, eat this meal every day. And I can assure you, while some items are an acquired taste, they are very effective. They will satisfy the soul's hunger for happiness.

What to Expect

I would like to point out that you will not see any prices on the menu. But that doesn't mean the meal will be free. It does require an investment on your part, which I think you'll find very affordable. However, when you receive the check at the end of the meal, you'll have the option to refuse payment if you think it's overpriced. I intend to passively present the information, leaving you to choose what you'd like to do with it. Again, I am not here to tell you what to do or what to believe. In other words, you will have the opportunity to dine and dash and this restaurant will be perfectly fine with it!

When I fully grasped these teachings, I was very skeptical that some of these simple things could really lead to ultimate happiness. After all, I was born in Missouri, whose slogan is the "Show Me" state. So, I needed to see it to believe it. Since I needed to experience it for myself, I encourage you to do the same. In fact, please don't believe me. Try them for yourself and prove them wrong. I assure you plenty of people have taken that challenge, only to find they actually do work.

You may find some of the courses are a little meatier than others. It is recommended that you chew your food well to aid in digestion. Since you are this restaurant's only reservation today, I encourage you to spend as much time on each of the courses as you feel you need.

Again, I discovered most teachings say virtually the same things, regardless of the foundational beliefs. But they do use very different terms. Simply put, they use different words to say basically the same things.

Let me illustrate what I mean. If you experience good fortune, are you lucky or blessed? Two different terms that can be used to describe the same thing but vary based on how you choose to look at it. If someone's out of their mind, are they crazy, nuts, bonkers, psychotic, mentally challenged, looney tunes or whacko? Again, very different terms that describe a similar mindset, yet vary depending on your perspective. Is one who is concerned about money frugal, greedy or a tight wad? Is one enlightened, wise, have an advanced level of consciousness or a higher energetic vibration?

Focus on terminology is actually the one thing that bothered me about corporate training programs. Just like these teachings, most sales training programs say the same things, but they use different terminology. Early in my career, I remember receiving a call from the gentleman who ran our company's "university". He told me we were replacing the SPIN Selling program with a new one called Professional Selling Skills. He said, "I know you are a huge SPIN advocate, but I really need you to be on board with this new program."

I told him, "Frankly, I don't care what program we use. I seem like a SPIN advocate only because I reinforce the program's terminology every chance I can. I do that because I want people to get past the words and be able to do it in their sleep. I suggest we pick one program and stay with it until it becomes a *skill* people can use to get results."

That is your goal in reading this book, correct? Results, right? Do you want to *know* how to be happy, in new words? Or do you want to actually *be* happy?

Changing terminology can confuse things and thus prevent us from developing a skill. Therefore, in this book I attempt to use terminology we can all relate to. I don't want you to get hung up on the words; I want you to understand the concepts. I'll also use a lot of analogies and examples to help make it clear. The menu is designed to be simple and easy to read, so you can focus on developing the skill of being happy. I truly want you to be able to do it in your sleep.

Being Happy is a Skill

There are a few things I feel like I know in this world, one of which is how we develop a skill. We don't take one singing class and leave capable of winning the next American Idol. Any skill takes practice.

There are basically two steps to developing a skill:

1. Learning the concepts (through repetition or reinforcement)
2. Practicing what you learned to become capable or experienced (through repetition, evaluation and adjustment)

A book called *Conversations with God* discusses a concept that supports what I discovered as a corporate trainer, regarding how we become skilled at anything. The concept is that of knowing, experiencing and being.

Assuming you drive, think about how you became a driver.

- Knowing—first you were a passenger for years and watched how other people did it, then maybe you took a Driver's Ed course or someone taught you the basics
- Experiencing—then you got behind the wheel, usually with someone who was brave enough to be in the car with you while you consciously focused on each step—starting the car, putting it in gear, checking the mirrors, using the blinkers, hands at 10 and 2, etc.
- Being—after enough practice you became a driver, hopefully a good one

My hope for you is to not only **know** how to be happy, but to actually **experience** happiness and **be** happy. Sound good?

Giving Thanks/Saying Grace

Before we dig in, I'd like to take a moment to give thanks and offer acknowledgements. Please allow me to express my gratitude to the following:

You—I would like to thank you for allowing me to share this meal with you today. I truly believe *experiencing* this meal will change you in more ways than you can imagine.

The Master Chefs who, for centuries, have been sharing the ingredients which make up this meal. While there are too many to list here, you will see some of them quoted throughout the menu. (Thanks to all of you for the repetition.)

The Restaurant Reviewers include *everyone* who has helped to create my life experiences thus far. Even though I may have enjoyed the good reviews, the bad reviews are the ones that contributed to my growth as a soul and as a human being. Therefore, I am extremely grateful for both.

The Satisfied Diners and their positive encouragement; without them you may not be reading this book today. (Scotty, you always called right when I'd begin to doubt myself. Thank you for your contagious enthusiasm. Cyndi, you truly are an Angel. Your love, friendship and support mean the world to me!)

My Catering Clients are the various groups who've allowed me to speak about this meal. This includes hospitals, schools and businesses. While I've enjoyed them all, I would like to acknowledge the group that truly warms my heart. They are the inmates serving in the Nevada Department of Corrections who've dined with me. (Ladies and Gentlemen, it's been such a pleasure getting to know you. I don't think you'll ever know the impact of your encouragement and support. Director Skolnik, without your forward thinking and progressive vision I would have never been blessed to meet and work with the souls serving under your watch. Thank you!)

Our Internal Hunger sent me on the journey to find a meal that would satisfy the soul.

My Personal Taste Tester—Life has a way of sending you exactly what, or who, you need even if you don't recognize it at the time. (Greg, thank you for holding the mirror; especially, when I really didn't want to look. You helped me to learn so much about myself. The reflection helped me see my beauty, my "flaws" and eventually the beauty in my "flaws". I will forever be grateful to you for this.)

This Soul's Delivery Service—my parents were the best delivery service I could have ever asked for. (Dad, thank you for the role you played in my life. You were always there to teach me when I was ready to learn. You challenged me when it was time for growth. I miss you so much, but somehow know you are still very present in my life. I hope you are still able to feel my love. Mom, although I've tried, I'm not sure words can ever really describe the magnitude of love and respect I have for you. You are such an amazing woman and I'm privileged to have you in my life! Thank you for everything.)

For their introduction to the Head Chef, I would like to thank Sri Ammabhagavan, Tony, Sage and the ODG's for the personal introduction to The Higher Power. How do you thank someone who does that for you? (My life is forever changed since the day you made that introduction. Thank you!!!!)

The Head Chef—God, Source, Jesus, Yahweh, Universal Energy, Allah, Giver of life, Buddha, Consciousness, Ishvara, Creator, Deus, Lord Almighty, Source, Higher Self, Shakti, Jehovah or Christ (First, thanks for not caring what name I choose to call you. I am grateful to have you as my newest and best friend. Thanks for being there all along, even when I was certain you didn't exist. Thank You so much for Life and the opportunity to *experience* it!)

Are you getting hungry? Please allow me to direct your attention to the menu.

Part 2

The Menu

The 1ˢᵗ Course

Think back to what you wished for in the one wish game—the thing that would make you happy.

Once your wish was granted, how long do you think it would make you happy?

Until the money was gone, until the love of your life cheated, until you aged and lost your hotness, until your children became teenagers possessed by hormones or until the next world war erupted?

Surely you remember something you wanted as a child. I'll bet you were certain if you just had that one thing, you'd be happy forever, right? Once you got it, what happened? Are you still feeling the happiness it brought you all those years ago? I know it sounds silly but this is part of the insanity we face as humans. It is how we function. We are just like we were as children—certain if we just had this one more thing it would bring us everlasting happiness.

And with the speed things are happening in society today, often our happiness doesn't even last as long as it did ten years ago. As society has sped up, so has our appetite. In many cases, we are immediately hungry for another wish.

No matter what we get, we don't stay full for long. It's like eating a meal with a lot of rice—you feel stuffed, but an hour later you're hungry again. It must have something to do with how quickly the rice digests.

This is the way human beings are. It is how we are built. We don't stay full for long, so we are always hungry.

Why We're Always Hungry

Do you remember Maslow and his hierarchy of needs? Well, it's very simple. You start at the base of the pyramid and move your way up.

5. Self-Actualization

4. Prestige

3. Love and Acceptance

2. Security

1. Basic needs for survival: Food, Clothing and Shelter

Once we're full of #1, we're hungry for #2.
Once we're full of #2, we're hungry for #3.
Once we're full of #3, we're hungry for #4.
Once we're full of #4, we're hungry for #5.

I was always a fan of Maslow, as he helped me understand at a very early age why we are always hungry for more. Concepts similar to Maslow's appear frequently in happiness teachings, using other terminology of course. I don't know which came first, Maslow's teachings or others. Since I'm not sure it matters, I never really cared enough to do the research to find out. Nonetheless, I want to highlight an example of how different terms can describe the same thing.

The Oneness University teaches a concept similar to Maslow's. They say our suffering varies between 3 areas:

Spiritual	=	Maslow's 5
Psychological	=	Maslow's 3 & 4
Physical	=	Maslow's 1 & 2

Bottom line: The first four leave us feeling hungry for more. If we can get our fill of number five, it is the only one that can satisfy our hunger.

So what's different about number five? Notice that the first four all depend on things and circumstances outside us. In other words, they come from our outside world.

"Happiness is not a state you arrive at (outside),
but a manner of traveling (inside)."
-Margaret Lee Runback (1905-1956)
American Author

This brings us to the first course of your Meal.

Accept that Ultimate Happiness is found in the Inside World

Now I can't speak for you, but I do get a positive feeling from material things, from feeling loved by another, from recognition, etc. And all those things come from the outside world. So, if that positive feeling isn't ultimate happiness, what is it? Many teachings call it pleasure. Pleasure feels really good at the time, but it is fleeting. Ultimate happiness is a joy that is not dependent on anything in the outside world, therefore it lasts.

"Happiness is not pleasure, it's victory."
-Zig Ziglar (Born 1926)
American Author & Motivational Speaker

Let's face it, finding freedom to be exactly who we are, is virtually impossible in the outside world. Everywhere we go, we are overwhelmed with what's wrong with us. Although, they don't say it exactly like that. It usually comes in disguise. We are told how we can be better. Marketing campaigns tell us to be thinner, sexier, have smoother skin, be healthier and wealthier, have whiter teeth, drive a better car, get a date, dress nicer, have more fun or more hair and be a better parent or lover. Pushing our "I'm not enough" button gets us to spend money in an attempt to *become enough*. And advertisers aren't the only ones who are telling us we can be more. Many religions tell us how we should be more virtuous. Our friends and families with the best of intentions tell us how to live. In fact some of you may read this book and see the teachings to be a new set of rules or standards by which to measure your life.

If we leave it up to the outside world, we will never be enough or have enough.

"You will never find liberation in the outside world."
-Sri Amma (Born 1954)
One of the Global visionaries behind Oneness

To further illustrate this, I'm sure you can name at least one celebrity or rock star that seems to have it all in the outside world. They have money, glamour and the finer things. They are loved and adored by millions. But many still aren't happy. How many stories like that can you think of that have tragic endings?

Conversely, having money, fame or other material things does not mean that you can't or won't be happy. You can be happy with tons of material things. You can be happy with few material things. The point is that material success is not the determining factor.

This is a very hard concept for many to embrace. With regard to material success, here are two common mindsets:

- Some think "People who have tons of money have absolutely nothing to complain about. Their lives are perfect. If I had millions, I'd be the happiest person in the world."
- Others believe, "If you want to be spiritual, you must live modestly and shun material success." We've all heard "money is the root of all evil."

"Happiness does not depend on outward things,
but on the way we see them."
-Count Leo Tolstoy (1828-1910)
Russian Nobility & Author of "War and Peace"

Money is not evil. It is our thoughts and beliefs about money which can cause us to crave it. This craving can lead to greed and/or hoarding. So *it's not material things in the outside world that determine our happiness. It's actually our thoughts and beliefs in our inner world that determine our happiness.*

"A happy person is not a person in a certain set of circumstances,
but rather a person with a certain set of attitudes."
-Hugh Downs (Born 1921)
American TV Broadcaster & Author

While ultimate happiness can't be obtained from the outside world, it is important to reinforce that it can't be withheld either. Meaning, if the situations or circumstances in your life can't give you true joy, they can't take it away either. Look back at my pre-merger experience. Everything was happy in my life, until my outside world changed. I didn't feel so happy in the new company's culture. What I thought was happiness was actually pleasure, since it was dependent on my life's situations and circumstances—in other words, my outside world.

"Your vision will become clear only when you can look into your own
heart. Who looks outside, dreams; who looks inside, awakes."
-Carl Jung (1875-1961)
Swiss Psychiatrist & Founder of Analytical Psychology

Accepting that your happiness comes from your inside world, independent of your life's situations, makes up the first course because it lays the foundation for everything else. According to Dr. David Hawkins, who is considered an authority on consciousness and enlightenment, says in his book *Power vs. Force* that only .4% of the world's population will experience this concept. Similarly, Maslow stated that 1% or less of the population would reach the top of the pyramid and become self-actualized.

Understanding this concept is pretty easy. Accepting it and experiencing it, are skills you will develop in time. You may be thinking, "I get it." Or, "I know this; it will be easy to apply in my life."

Just wait until the next time someone cuts you off in traffic or your boss reprimands you for something. See how happy you feel. Vice versa, see how long the pleasure lasts after receiving a bonus or after someone helps you out of a tight spot.

So what is it that we get from our inner world that allows us to find a joy that sustains us, no matter what's going on in our life? Teaching after teaching points to an amazing power we all have inside of us.

"What lies behind us, what lies before us,
are tiny matters compared to what lies within us."
-Ralph Waldo Emerson (1803-1882)
American Philosopher & Poet

"An aim in life is the only fortune worth finding; and it is not to be
found in foreign lands, but in the heart itself."
-Robert Louis Stevenson (1850-1894)
Scottish Poet & Writer

"If you don't go within, you go without."
Conversations with God (1995)

Buddhism also speaks to this power within. Buddha literally means "the awakened one"—someone who has no ignorance and can see the universe as it really is. People who have achieved this state can be called a Buddha. In other words, we all have a Buddha inside of us that can be awakened.

"The Kingdom of God is within you."
-Luke 17:21

When we tap into this power that lies within us, we have the ability to then change our outside world. Once you go within, you begin to change the way you see things, which then determines what you experience in your life. When you feel happy on the inside, more happy things happen in the outside world. This is popularly referred to as manifesting.

I heard a six year old describe it this way, "Every thought is a prayer." That may be a frightening prospect for some. Imagine, you've been thinking, "Life sucks!" And The Higher Power says, "Ok, if you say so. And so it shall be!"

Physics calls it the "Law of Attraction". Everything in the outside, including our bodies, is made of atoms (energy) and our thoughts and emotions also have an energetic vibration.

*"On such things as matter we have all been wrong, what we have
called matter is energy, whose vibration has been so
lowered as to be perceptible to the senses.
There is no matter."*
-Albert Einstein (1879-1955)
Physicist & Philosopher, Nobel Prize in Physics (1921)

EEG's read the brain's energetic activity. Our thought and
emotional vibrations attract things and circumstances which are
at the same vibration. In other words, the energetic vibration from
happiness in your inside world attracts more positive experiences
to make you happy in your outside world.

"The outside world is a reflection of the inside world "
-Sri Bhagavan (Born 1949)
Spiritual Leader & Founder of Oneness University

"What's going on in the inside shows on the outside."
-Earl Nightingale (1921-1989)
American Motivational Speaker

*"He, who cannot change the very fabric of his thought,
will never be able to change his reality."*
-Anwar Sadat (1918-1981)
3rd President of Egypt

*"The greatest revolution of our generation is that of human beings,
who, by changing the inner attitudes of their minds,
can change the outer aspects of their lives."*
-Marilyn Ferguson (1938-2008)
American Author & Public Speaker

Numerous random number generator experiments have
proven that intention affects the outcome time and time again.
So, for the science minded diners: mind is over matter.

I think of it like a magic bow & arrow that we use to create our
lives. And it works whether we know how to use it or not. You aim
the bow with your thoughts. The power is determined by how far
you pull the string & arrow back. This is done with the intensity of

your emotion. So, let's say you have a thought that, "Life is difficult," and you have a lot of intense emotion about how difficult your life has been. The thought means you are aiming at difficulty and the intensity of your emotion has you pulling the arrow back pretty far. Therefore, you'll be attracting more difficulty, with a lot of power. On the other hand, if your thoughts are focused on being successful and you are very passionate about it, you'll easily attract success. The bow & arrow has been working your whole life even if you didn't know it or know how to use it.

Please take a moment to make note of what you think about with intense emotion. List the thought and the emotion.

Thought (what you think)	**Emotion (how you feel)**

How are those thoughts and emotions affecting what you are attracting in your life?

_____

_____

_____

_____

_____

_____

_____

_____

_____

The challenge for most human beings is that we tend to think more about what we don't want. For example, if someone is very worried (power) about a poor financial situation (target) he'd actually be attracting more of the same.

If you wanted a more positive outcome, how might you use your bow & arrow more effectively? Remember to focus on what you WANT rather than what you DON'T want.

Thought (aiming at)	Emotion (power)

There's a relatively popular movie and book called *The Secret* that explains this topic in a simple, yet more detailed fashion if you'd like to learn more.

Maybe your bow & arrow is working just fine and everything in your life is going pretty well. Maybe you have loved ones that are suffering, or you are feeling challenged by others in some way. Even if you feel it's your mission to help save others from their suffering, your first step in doing so is going within you, not them.

> *"Everyone thinks of changing the world, but no one thinks of changing himself."*
> *-Count Leo Tolstoy (1828-1910)*
> *Russian Nobility & Author of "War and Peace"*

By changing your internal world, you can change your outer world. Since other people are in your outer world, that means if you grow, others around you will also grow with no additional effort on your part. Change in the outer world happens because everything around us is connected energetically. I was very skeptical of this at first. However, I have experienced this and witnessed an obvious change in another person when I grew. When we truly focus on our inside world, the growth happens and people around us change—or at least our experience of them changes.

Oneness

What *is* this power we are able to connect to inside of us? Some say it's God. Some call it Buddha. Others refer to it as our higher self. Whatever you call it, we all have access to it. In fact, we are all connected, whether we are aware of it or not. We are all parts of a whole.

> *"All are but parts of one stupendous whole,*
> *whose body nature is, and God the soul."*
> *"An Essay on Man"* (1734)

> *"And mankind is naught but a single nation."*
> -Holy Quran, 2:213

Let me use a technology example to illustrate. Individually, we can use computers to do some pretty cool stuff: build spreadsheets, create presentations, write letters, retouch photos, etc. But when we connect to the internet, we can download music, do research, shop for just about anything, find new recipes, market a business, gamble, rent movies, lookup a phone number and even find a date. The options of the internet seem almost limitless. And what is the internet exactly? It's a web of computers that are connected to one another. This is an example of Oneness. Each human being is like a computer—we can do some pretty amazing things. But when we connect, join forces or tap into our Oneness, like the internet we can do so much more.

Since humans have within us the power to manifest, attract or create things, imagine the power that we have when we join forces. Miracles can happen. This is also referred to in the Bible.

> *"Where two or three have come together in my name,*
> *I am there among them."*
> -Matthew 18:20

Additionally, there have been studies on the effectiveness/power of group prayer, showing that the focused intention of a group affects the outcome.

Not into all the spiritual stuff? Scientists are saying the same thing. Entanglement is the scientific term which describes the

Oneness phenomenon. Erwin Schrödinger, one of the founders of quantum mechanics called "Entanglement" the defining trait of quantum theory. Einstein famously dubbed it Spukhafte Fernwirkungen or "spooky action at a distance".

> *"Connectivity among all things is a*
> *basic constituent to the fabric of reality."*
> —Dean Radin (Born 1952)
> *Laboratory Scientist, Researcher & Author*

I'm sure you've experienced our connectedness on some level. Have you ever thought about someone you haven't spoken to in some time, and then they call you within a few days? Or have you called someone and they said they were just going to call you? You were connected through thoughts or feelings before you were connected in a conversation. This is an example of Oneness.

> *"Our separation from each other is*
> *an optical illusion of consciousness."*
> -Albert Einstein (1879-1955)
> *Physicist & Philosopher, Nobel Prize in Physics (1921)*

Some teachings state that our unhappiness comes directly from our sense of separation, rather than a sense of Oneness. Is it possible that our collective unhappiness in our inside world is manifesting/creating what we are experiencing in the outside world today—in our environment and our economy? Could it be affecting our health? I'm not here to tell you what to believe. I do, however, think it's worth a few moments of our consideration.

Note some of your thoughts about connectedness, or Oneness.

How does feeling separate affect your happiness?

---

*"When our focus is toward a principle
of relatedness and oneness . . . health ensues."*
-Larry Dossey, M.D. (Born 1940)
Internist, Author & Lecturer

The human body is another wonderful example of Oneness. There are so many components in our bodies and the way they relate, or work together, affects our health and well-being. If any one part goes out of balance we can be affected somewhere else in our body. Because everything affects something else—this affects that, which affects something else, and so on. This is Oneness.

Many believe we are truly at a unique time in human evolution. More and more people are having experiences that make it clear that we are not only connected to one another, we are connected to all life.

I had a glimpse of our Oneness after one of our nation's most tragic events, September 11, 2001. Amidst all our suffering in the days following, I was overwhelmed with the beauty I saw in our unity. For those few days, we had compassion for our fellow man. We stopped judging each other and stood united. We were Americans. It was very unfortunate that so many had to lose their lives in order for us to stop and love our neighbors. While it may be difficult to see the beauty in such a horrible tragedy, nonetheless, that is what Oneness feels like—compassion for all life.

Imagine feeling that on a global scale. Some say that as we evolve as a species we will experience this in our lifetime.

If you're tasting this course for the first time, please allow plenty of time for digestion. Since it's the foundation of your soul's meal, it may help to revisit this part of the menu multiple times and contemplate its flavors.

Summary

1st Course **Accept that Ultimate Happiness is Found in the Inside World**

The 2nd Course

This course may seem like a bit of a contradiction, considering the proposed outcome of ultimate happiness. I appreciate your openness as we explore the second course of your meal.

Accept ALL Feelings & Emotions

Understanding this one can take some time.

We all have negative thoughts that bring about feelings like fear, jealousy, anger, frustration, etc. And every human being who has walked the face of this earth has experienced these emotions, including Jesus, Buddha, Krishna, Mohammed, Abraham, saints, sages and enlightened masters. In fact, embracing all of who we are, including these negative emotions, can be a propellant towards ultimate happiness or enlightenment.

> *"Not to have felt pain is not to have been human."*
> *-Jewish Proverb*

Some teachings say those thoughts/emotions *do not* keep us from ultimate happiness. What keeps us from being happy are our judgments of those thoughts and emotions. Again, what keeps us from being happy is our *judgment* of our thoughts and emotions.

> *"Man's biggest problem is labeling things, a problem."*
> *-Sri Bhagavan (Born 1949)*
> *Spiritual Leader & Founder of Oneness University*

The way our mind works can be compared to the most awesome filing system ever. It categorizes and labels everything, so that it can be filed. Everything the mind takes in is labeled with many different distinctions like what it is, color, size, shape, texture, etc. These are what we consider facts. We learned the names of things, standards of measure and colors as a means of communication. For example, how do you know what a stop sign is? You learned it from someone else, likely an adult, right? You learned that it is an octagon, that it's red and white, and that it has letters that form the word stop. You also learned what you are supposed to do when you approach one of these signs. The mind is very helpful when it comes to functioning in a world with other people. If we all agree to stop at a stop sign, it helps us to move in an orderly fashion.

Once the facts are identified, the mind moves to more categories and labels we call opinions or beliefs. An easy way to think about a belief is that it takes a thought and attaches an emotion to it. This is often referred to as an emotional charge. That is why we appear to be emotionally attached to these ideas called beliefs.

Is it good, bad, right, wrong, pretty, ugly, rude, polite, smart, stupid, better, worse, a sin, virtuous, loving, hateful, etc? Notice that all of these are opposites. Some people rely heavily on these polarities, generally referred to as black or white in their thinking. Some opinions can vary by degree anywhere in between, and are often considered shades of gray. But make no mistake, regardless of the degree, beliefs can create miracles or start world wars.

> *"Beliefs have the power to create and the power to destroy."*
> *-Anthony Robbins (Born 1960)*
> *American Self-Help Author & Motivational Speaker*

How do we know if something is right or wrong? Our thoughts and beliefs tell us. We like to think that our beliefs are our own, but we also learned many of them from adults. We learned what *they* thought was right, wrong, good and bad. We often learned them through an emotionally charged experience.

> *"Nothing is good or bad, but thinking makes it so."*
> *-William Shakespeare (1564-1616)*
> *English Poet & Playwright*

When we arrive in this world, we are primarily emotional in our being. We have an intrinsic expectation that we will receive unconditional love. And many of us get it. Our parents' brains are producing a lot of oxytocin, sometimes referred to as the "love hormone". Oxytocin helps our parents love us unconditionally. We can do no wrong in their eyes. We cry & spew bodily functions on them and they gush over how cute we are in the process. Their minds are drunk with unconditional love. Everything is right in our world. Then . . . the "love hormone" production returns to normal; the mind sobers up and returns to normal functioning. What a rude awakening that must be for an emotional being to encounter the mind. Some refer to this first encounter as the original sin.

As we grow, these loving beings we had come to know begin to give us a new experience. When we do something they think is wrong, we are met with other emotions like frustration and anger. Through this process, we begin to learn that there are things we do that cause us to feel loved and other things we do that make us feel unloved.

You're perfect as you are = unconditional love
Be different = conditional love

In other words, we learned that love has conditions. Conditions that come from what our parents/adults think. When adults praised us for what they thought was *good* behavior, it gave us a *good* feeling. We felt loved. The way adults treated us when we were *bad* gave us an emotional charge, which taught most of us that being good was our better option if we wanted love in return. Our mind records these conditions that get love and the conditions that don't get love. Our logic and reason kick in somewhere around 6 yrs. old, not coincidentally when we are sent to first grade. By that age our subconscious has already been programmed with plenty of adult conditions. We then spend the rest of our lives trying to meet those conditions, so we can get what we intrinsically expect—love. Incidentally, this is another thing we all have in common. We all want to be happy and we all want to be loved.

"We forfeit three-fourths of ourselves to be like other people."
-Arthur Schopenhauer (1788-1860) German Philosopher

So, life becomes about manipulation. We alter what we do, how we act and who we are, in order to fit in, be accepted and get love.

Have you ever done all the right things in a relationship and still not received love? Have you ever said something like, "I have done everything for you and you still don't treat me right"? Translation: "I have met all the conditions programmed in my subconscious and you haven't." As you can see from the translation, we place many of those same conditions on others in order to feel good about giving love.

Through this same kind of conditioned learning we were taught that fear, anger, jealousy, frustration, etc. were *bad* emotions, or emotions we should not have. As children, when we were having a temper tantrum we still wanted unconditional love. When our negative emotions were not met with a loving reception, our subconscious mind recorded this as yet another condition. The negative emotion was the condition we did not meet in order to get a loving response.

Today, our subconscious mind continues to operate from a basis of conditional love. Our mind tells us we must be a certain way in order to get love and that others must be a certain way to get love from us. This concept alone continues to affect our lives in more ways than we can imagine.

Since most of us want to be a good person (because we usually felt more love when we were good and less love when we were bad) we learned to avoid these negative emotions. In other words we learned to *resist* a natural part of our human experience. Remember, every human being has felt these emotions. So we are resisting or suppressing part of who we are, in an attempt to get love, approval and acceptance. Because we believe "good people *deserve* those things and bad people don't".

"People deny reality. They fight against real feelings caused by real circumstances. They build mental worlds of shoulds, oughts and might have beens. Real changes begin with real appraisals and acceptance of what is. Then realistic action is possible."
-Michael Crichton (1942-2008) American Writer & Filmmaker

Let's look at an example of how most men in our society have been conditioned. What is the first thought you have when you picture a man crying? Ever hear the saying big boys don't cry? I have heard many heartbreaking stories from men about the negative consequences that were inflicted upon them as boys when they cried. Let's face it, it's far more acceptable for a woman to cry than a man. Is it possible that men have a shorter life expectancy because of this one conditioned response to resist crying? Is it possible that allowing women to get some of the emotion out actually prolongs health? That may be something to consider.

"Suffering is the incapacity to experience things as they are."
-Sri Bhagavan (Born 1949)
Spiritual Leader & Founder of Oneness University

The Judgment and our attempts to avoid *what is,* is commonly referred to as resistance in various teachings. Most say that our resistance is the true cause of our suffering, not the emotion itself.

"Happiness is a continuation of happenings which are not resisted."
-Deepak Chopra (Born 1946)
American Physician, born in India

Other teachings actually perpetuate our desire to avoid our negative emotions. They teach all sorts of techniques on how to change your emotions. While I subscribed to that school of thought for years, I must tell you I feel far better when I allow all my emotions. It is far easier to accept them and allow them to pass than to spend so much energy fighting them off and beating myself up for having them. I believe this contradiction in the teachings comes from a misunderstanding in how we *experience* our emotions. We'll discuss this further, later in your meal.

Let's look at the concept of *acceptance* from another angle. Are you bothered by gravity? Do you lose sleep at night because you can't float around? Doesn't it just tic you off? Or are you completely peeved that the sun comes up over the east horizon instead of the west? I know it sounds ridiculous, but can you imagine how unhappy you would feel if your mind's evaluation was "it's wrong; it should be different"? Can you imagine the quality of a man's life if he witnessed what his mind labeled a travesty every single day? Would you agree that resisting something as natural as gravity or how the earth rotates in relation to the sun would certainly affect one's happiness?

Doesn't it make sense that a good part of our unhappiness is actually coming from resisting our very nature—our human nature?

What emotions do you avoid? What emotions do you think are unproductive?

_____

_____

_____

_____

_____

_____

_____

_____

_____

_____

This course of our meal could also be called:
- Accept yourself as you are, good, bad and otherwise.
- Accept all of you, including your negative thoughts and emotions
- Love all of you, including your negative tendencies
- Pretending like you're only good, doesn't make it so

"Heroes became heroes, flaws and all.
You don't have to be perfect to fulfill your dream."
-Peter McWilliams (1949-2000)
American Self-Help Author

"Growth is not measured by the amount of joy or love you experience
every day or how many times you experienced God or how long
you experienced thoughtlessness. If at all, it is measured by how
comfortable you are with yourself; with your fear; with your
nervousness; with your frustration, that is growth."
-Sri Anandagiri (Born 1976)
Spiritual Teacher, World Oneness Academy

The judgments and resistance we have toward our negative thoughts and emotions are responsible for causing more pain than the actual emotions themselves. Meaning, *running* from a negative emotion requires far more energy and causes more pain than the actual emotion itself, when allowed to run its course. If instead we experience the emotion, it passes fairly quickly and leaves our body. Our resistance actually suppresses the emotion, causing us to carry it around. I now look at the term emotional baggage in a whole new way.

"Any negative emotion that is not fully faced and seen for what it is in the moment it arises does not completely dissolve.
It leaves behind a remnant of pain."
-Eckhart Tolle (Born 1948)
German Writer & Spiritual Teacher

"Emotions have to do with survival. The human being lives in a cultural cage inhibited by the norms and dictates of the institutions of the culture, that don't allow that kind of behavior or restrict its ability to express itself. And all of these animals are subject to a variety of emotional and physical complaints and illnesses based on their inability to discharge the (response)."
-Robert Scaer, M.D. (Born 1938)
Neurologist who lectures on trauma

Dr. Scaer goes on to explain that when the body is not allowed to complete its trauma cycle, our vulnerability and resiliency are affected. Our resiliency to trauma goes down, making us more susceptible to future traumas. Again, we are more susceptible to future traumas.

Many spiritual teachings also point to the idea that emotional traumas from our childhood will continue to resurface throughout our entire lives. We will have to keep dealing with it over and over. Each time it resurfaces, and we resist it, we only delay the inevitable. It will keep coming back until you stop resisting and fully experience the feelings that arise in you, even if your mind is uncomfortable with the label.

"What you resist persists."
-Carl Jung (1875-1961)
Swiss Psychiatrist & Founder of Analytical Psychology

What is one negative emotion that seems to keep resurfacing in your life or in your relationships?

_____

_____

_____

_____

This seems to be the great cosmic joke. In order to be free from something that's negative, we must first accept it exactly as it is. Our acceptance of it seems to diminish its power. The harder we struggle against it, the more power it drains from us.

Many teachings suggest that we experience, or allow all the emotions that arise in us.

I must tell you, it worked for me just like they say. But, I did struggle a bit with what it means to *experience* the emotion. How are we supposed to *experience* anger? Scream, yell and throw things? Calmly talk with our offender about how wrong they are? No. Why aren't those options the most effective? These options are *outside* us. As you recall from the first course, ultimate happiness starts with the inside world. You *feel* the emotion inside, without judgment. We'll discuss this further in the fourth course.

Speaking of the inside world, what about the emotional baggage we are all carrying? Yes, we are all carrying emotional baggage, whether we choose to acknowledge it or not. Every time we've resisted an emotion, it was put into our emotional suitcase. Since this baggage is very heavy, it takes a lot of energy to lug it all around. When we carry it around with us, it continues to cause us problems. It makes our back hurt or we can become afflicted with various other physical ailments or dis-ease.

If you were around adults at all as a child, you have emotional baggage. They are the ones who taught us to resist. By adults, I mean parents, older siblings, teachers, baby sitters, TV adults, and church adults; all of whom were well meaning. After all, they were just passing on what they learned from the adults in their life, in an attempt to prepare us for the world. This cycle of learning resistance has been passed from generation to generation for years.

Now, if you are swearing up and down that you don't have any baggage. I know where you're at. That was me.

"We must re-explore what we define as trauma,
especially in infancy and childhood."
-Robert Scaer, M.D. (Born 1938)
Neurologist who lectures on trauma

I had a relatively good childhood. While we weren't rich, I still had food, clothes, lived in a nice neighborhood and had plenty of opportunities. Any parts of my childhood that weren't perfect or seemed hard at the time, actually helped me develop qualities which came to serve me well in life. For example, my parents divorced when I was eight. My primary caretaker was a single mother who worked, which gave me plenty of time alone as a child. This actually helped me to become independent and a great problem solver. Like my time alone, I had become grateful for everything in my childhood, including the imperfect. I really didn't have much tolerance for people who spent a lot of time blaming their childhood for why they weren't happy as an adult. In fact, one of my favorite sayings was, "Shame on my parents for who I am today, but shame on me for staying that way." I still enjoy the saying, but look at it in a whole new way.

I discovered the logic and understanding I'd come to as an adult did not serve me at the emotional level. This was actually another way to avoid *experiencing* the loneliness baggage I'd felt as a child. Since I'd reached a level of gratitude for the good that had come from being alone as a child, the mind convinced me there was no reason or condition that little girl should have felt lonely. But soon after I began looking inward, it became clear: no matter how great the outcome from being alone, I was still carrying some pain that came from that little girl's loneliness. Again, logic, reason and understanding actually interfered with the ability to experience the emotion. Since there were benefits, the mind labeled and filed it as a good experience. Case closed.

If you still doubt that you are carrying any emotional baggage, ask yourself this question. Is there any part of you that feels like you're not enough?

- not smart enough
- not attractive enough
- not young enough
- not old enough
- not funny enough
- not grateful enough
- not successful enough
- not giving enough
- not virtuous enough
- not kind enough
- not a good enough parent
- not enough

This is our mind telling us why we are not deserving of love or ultimate happiness. We're not meeting the conditions of the mind, conscious or subconscious.

None of those ring true for you? Have you ever known someone who could really push your buttons? Usually the button pusher is someone who's gotten close to you—or at least close enough to know what buttons to push. Sometimes it may be someone with whom you've had a brief encounter, where the person wasn't even trying to push them but hit one by accident. Airline employees were my button pushers when I was traveling frequently. Regardless, if you have ever been bothered, annoyed or frustrated with another human being, you have emotional baggage. The buttons are your baggage. If you have buttons, you have baggage. It's not so bad really—you are a human being, just like the rest of us.

You are a human being who has learned to resist parts of your nature in order to meet some perceived conditions to be worthy of love. We then place these learned conditions on others. When met, we give love. We withhold love if someone isn't treating us right. How do you know what your conditions or rules are? Ask yourself, what does it mean to "treat you right"?

_____

_____

_____

_____

_____

_____

_____

_____

_____

_____

_____

_____

_____

As you were writing, did you find the mind justifying its beliefs about what it means for someone to treat you right? "That's not too much to ask, is it?" "I think anyone would agree with me on this, right?" Take notice of how the mind supports itself and its beliefs.

If you are a parent, you may be feeling a little anxiety while wondering how you might be affecting your child(ren). Take a deep breath. It's ok. Parents will help their children learn some of the "rules" needed to function well in today's society. If the child is under 6 years old, he/she will likely store some emotional baggage. It's inevitable. However, now that you are armed with this knowledge, you can encourage your child to allow their negative emotions to move through them a little more often, and save some "rules" until they are a little older. Now, if you're pretty sure the damage is already done, relax. The rest of your meal is going to help you learn how to release some of your stored emotions, some of which are buried so deep you'd swear they don't exist.

"First mend yourself, then others."
-Jewish Proverb

Once you release some of your stored emotional charges, you'll be better equipped to help them release some of theirs. I truly believe we are all going to be ok, if we commit to letting go of our own baggage first. Think about the instructions you get on a plane, "For those of you traveling with small children, secure your oxygen mask first." You have to be ok, before you can most effectively help another.

Bottom line, the second course is about accepting yourself exactly as you are. Exactly as you are, right here, right now.

"Self-approval and self-acceptance in the now are
the keys to positive change."
-Louise Hay (Born 1926)
American Author & Founder of Hay House Publishing

"Perhaps the most important thing we can undertake toward the
reduction of fear is make it easier for people to accept themselves, to
like themselves."
-Bonaro Overstreet (1902-1985)
American Author & Leader in the fields of Child & Adult Education
& Mental Health

Until we can accept ourselves exactly where we are today, at the beginning of this journey, we will be challenged to reach the place of ultimate happiness.

"Every journey begins where you are, not where you are going."
-Sri Bhagavan (Born 1949)
Spiritual Leader & Founder of Oneness University

Let's use the analogy of a journey from Phoenix to New York. Phoenix is where you stand today. New York, like ultimate happiness, is where you want to go. How would your trip be affected if you swore up and down you were starting in Palm Springs? What would happen if your mind was insisting you were in Seattle? There you are standing in Phoenix, looking at a map of Seattle trying to figure out how to get to New York. Ridiculous, right?

The point is if you do not accept where you really are today, how do you know where the journey starts? On a cross country trip, you have no problem accepting where you are. It's not good, bad or otherwise. It is what it is. You are in Phoenix. When it comes to your personal life journey, all the mind's labels regarding the "type of person you are" can end up clouding your view. Be aware, your mind may try to convince you that you're in Seattle.

"A human being is born an absolute egoist; this quality is so visceral that it can convince him that he has already become righteous and has rid himself of all egoism."
-Talmud, Hagiga

I like to refer to this as our spiritual blind spot, or our ego's blind spot. We can always clearly see the mistakes others are making in their lives. Yet this blind spot prevents us from seeing many of our own mistakes.

The mind and ego tell us we're okay. It says, "That's not you. You've done all this work on yourself. I do love and accept myself. I've already faced and overcome my issues, so this doesn't apply to me. You used to feel that way but you have moved past it. But I do know someone who really needs these teachings; that's who needs to read this."

Where is your mind saying you are? Is it still resisting the idea that you even have any emotional baggage? Is it telling you that you're fine and it's others who are preventing you from reaching ultimate happiness?

_____

_____

_____

_____

_____

_____

_____

_____

_____

The next two courses are going to focus on how to allow and experience all of who you are, including your negative thoughts and emotions; the ones that happen in your day-to-day life, as well as the ones you have been carrying for years.

<u>Summary</u>

1st Course **Accept that Ultimate Happiness Begins in the Inside World**

2nd Course **Accept ALL Feelings & Emotions**

The 3rd Course

If we are going to work on really accepting and loving ourselves, we should probably get to know who we really are and how we arc.

"Know thyself."
-Socrates (469 BC—399 BC)
Greek Philosopher

This course in your meal asks us to take a deeper look at how the mind functions. First, it's important to understand that the mind functions the same for all of us, with few exceptions. While the mind functions the same for all of us, the content varies by individual. Let me use another internet example. Millions of people use Internet Explorer and it works in the same manner regardless of the user. However when we look at content, the websites a user visits, it's completely unique based on the individual. Our mind is the program and like Internet Explorer, it operates in the same way. Our thoughts are the content and are individual, just like the websites visited by each user.

Understanding that the mind functions the same way for all of us helped me learn my most important lesson about the mind: most of our challenges arise from functionality, rather than the content or stories that run through it. This is quite contrary to what most of us believe. Most of us think we are completely unique and that no one has the same problems we do. While the content or stories are completely unique, the mind's functionality is the same. You'll begin to see that our problems come more from function than content. As you take this in, you'll begin to see that your life challenges are more similar to others than different. In fact, after working with inmates, I can assure you we have more in common with convicted felons than you might ever imagine. At the core of our problems is the mind; and the content, while unique, is not very relevant. We will continue to revisit this throughout this course of your meal.

We've already covered the mind's amazing filing capabilities. It is also able to recall information from the files to help us problem solve, make decisions, find the words to communicate and function with other human beings. This is why I consider the mind one of our most valuable tools.

It also provides us with a running commentary on life that is virtually non-stop. The mind does so much for us and it likes us to constantly be aware of the workload. So it keeps talking to let us know when it's on the clock. It wants us to know its value. In fact, the mind has talked so much and so long that over time we have come to believe that is who we are. We can barely hear our own voice because the chatter of the mind is so incessant. It is constantly voicing opinions/beliefs/judgments, which we come to accept as *our* opinions/beliefs. In reality those opinions are merely being pulled from the filing system. And remember the subconscious part of our mind recorded opinions we heard from adults before we even developed logic and reason. When we were only emotional in our being, the mind filed everything it heard as facts. In other words, the opinions you've come to know as your own may not really be yours after all.

Those beliefs determine how we look at the world. We compare the way things are to the way our beliefs/judgments say it should be. The mind reports to us the difference between how things and people are, compared to how they should be. The more emotionally attached we are to the belief of *how it should be*, the greater our resistance or discomfort. This discomfort comes in the form of feelings we don't think we are supposed to have. So, we resist them. We try not to waste our time on negative emotions. Again, our mind is a wonderful tool but letting it run our lives without awareness of how it operates can be a bit risky.

"The mind is its own place, and in itself can make
a heaven of hell, a hell of heaven."
-John Milton (1608-1674)

Most of us in the United States live lives that would be considered heaven to those who are starving around our world. Yet our minds can still see hell in our experience. This is part of the nature of the human mind.

I know this may be a lot of new information for you to consider, so before we go any further, let me introduce this course of your meal.

Observe the Mind

While I'm going to share with you some of the observations I've made, this is a course that you must taste for yourself. I promise you'll be amazed at some of what you'll find. Again, please don't take my word for it; dig in and try it for yourself.

One of the things that surprised me most was that the mind seems to operate as if it's made up of different personalities. That doesn't mean we are schizophrenic, but there are definitely different personalities in there having a conversation. You'll have the inquisitive personality, the skeptic, the defiant one, the bored one, the loving nurturer, the angry one, the know-it-all, the bossy one, the optimist, etc. Since they are different, they don't always agree. Please take a moment to listen to the commentary that is happening right now. Before turning the page, please stop and ask yourself to observe your thoughts about what you just read.

What did the mind have to say?

_____

_____

_____

_____

It may have sounded something like this:
- Different personalities? What on earth is this woman saying?
- Is she saying I have split personalities?
- That's crazy.
- I think she's crazy.
- Wait a minute. I am starting to hear the running commentary she's talking about.
- Wow. Maybe there is something to this.
- I think it's ridiculous. Of course the voice I'm hearing is me. Who else would it be?

- Do you really care about this?
- If it can make me happier, I'll try it.
- How on earth is this going to make me happier? Please!
- Well, how am I becoming aware of this? If I am the thinker, how am I observing myself think?
- Maybe I am the observer, and not the thinker. Is that possible?
- No. Shut up and go back to reading. I don't want to think about this anymore.
- I don't want to shut up. I want to observe a little longer. This is kind of cool.
- No, it's not; it's stupid.

It may have sounded like that or it may have been completely different. You may have even had a bit of a challenge even understanding what it means to observe your mind.

Another way to look at these various personalities is like this: think of yourself as the owner of a company called Your Life. You have hired a board of directors to run your company, so you let them run it. When you begin observing the mind and its thoughts, I liken it to walking into the boardroom for the very first time. You get to walk in and see how these board members have been running Your Life. And please don't be surprised to find that most of them don't agree and many of them don't even get along. So, if you want to get more out of your company Your Life, it's time for you to see how things have really been running. You'll want to observe the board members to identify the strengths and weaknesses of each. Initially, you'll find yourself judging them and see them judge each other. Yes, the mind judges itself, interestingly enough.

By observing, you can pay attention to how your mind works and the conflicts that exist within it. It's not as easy as it sounds, because observing means staying impartial. You may think you are impartial or that you can be impartial, but the mind won't allow it. You are judgmental. You are a human being, whose nature is judgmental. Like I said, this will be apparent when you feel like firing board members left and right. "That one is too lazy. That one is too negative; all I hear is his complaining. That lady never shuts up."

Looks like this is a great opportunity to see how well you digested the last course. Are you comfortable embracing all of who you are, including the judgmental part of you? Did you feel any resistance when I called you judgmental in the last paragraph? Again, the mind is really the judgmental one, if that makes you feel any better. I always say to people who resist their judgmental nature, "If you want to stop being judgmental, you'll have to lose your mind." Most choose to keep their mind for the time being and move one step closer to accepting the mind is judgmental.

What is the mind saying to you about its judgmental nature?

_____

_____

_____

As you begin to accept the nature of the mind, you'll move one step further from the idea that the mind is *all* you are. Remember, the very nature of our mind is to make judgments— label, categorize and form opinions. If you choose to believe you are the thoughts the mind feeds you, then you are judgmental. This topic can be a mentally exhausting work out on its own. So for now, let's continue to assume you are the thinker. Your thoughts and opinions are your own.

I know there are plenty of you over achievers out there who are thinking, "I can remain completely impartial." So, you will set out to observe without judging. Notice, you will be judging yourself for judging. It goes something like this:

- I wonder what I'll have for dinner.
- See, that wasn't a judgment.
- I knew I'd be good at this.
- Wait, I said good. That's a judgment isn't it?
- Wow, you already made a judgment and you just started.
- Maybe you aren't going to be very good at this.
- Wait, not very good is another judgment.
- Crap, I can't believe I did it again.
- Wait, did I just judge myself for judging?
- What am I doing? I'm a good person, I don't judge.
- Did I say good person? Another judgment
- I am not a judgmental person.
- Another judgment, shoot!
- What's wrong with me?
- Did I say wrong, that's a judgment too!

- I can't believe it, I suck at this.
- Another judgment!
- Forget this!! It's ridiculous. Another judgment!
- I'm over this stupid exercise. It's a waste of time.
- I know. Another judgment.
- I'm going to get something to eat.

I am intrigued by how many of us resist our judgmental nature; as if swearing it doesn't exist will somehow take it away. Many are emotionally attached to how non-judgmental they are. For those who accept that they are judgmental, most are committed to changing it. Most of us have learned that being judgmental is something we don't want to be. So, the mind decides to commit to changing it—changing itself.

The mind, its stories and its judgments are responsible for our suffering. Then we seek distractions to avoid the result—an uncomfortable emotion or feeling. Realizing this, you may want to change your mind. In fact, the mind is the only part of us that thinks it's powerful enough to change itself. This is a nature of the mind. If you want to change your mind, accept it as it is in its current state. Remember the great cosmic joke, accepting something diminishes its power. Observe it. Observation is the first step on the road to acceptance. It's time to get to know the board members of Your Life!

Anything observed is changed.
-The Observer Effect, a principle of physics

At first, observing will be mentally exhausting workouts because you are trying to observe and think at the same time. As you continue to practice, your mind will become fatigued. Then you'll be able to observe you're judging without judging it. You just get tired of trying to fight it. You truly begin to accept how the mind operates and how we operate.

"The best thing you can do is get good at being you."
-Dennis the Menace (First appeared 1951)
British Comic Strip Character

I call it the "mental hamster wheel". In the last example, after sixty seconds, we were ready to get off the wheel and go eat. The most amazing transformation happens if you stay on.

Just like working out, growth occurs when you work a muscle to fatigue. Real growth occurs in your life, when you can work your mind to fatigue by observing it. Once you log enough time on the mental hamster wheel, your mind is able to see its own lunacy and gives up. It says, "Fine. I was tired of telling you what to do all the time. I'd rather just be a problem solving tool anyway." It begins to slowly relax and give you moments of peace. Over time the urgency to remind you of all its rules and conditions gradually diminishes.

How long do you have to stay on the hamster wheel? There is no hard answer to this. You stay on until your mind gets tired of itself. Until it gets tired enough to give up and just accept the way it is. It will strongly depend on how much you pay attention to your thoughts.

The good news is you don't have to log the laps on the hamster wheel. Your mind does. All you have to do is watch the mind do all the work, until it gets tired and sees its own ridiculousness. Once we see it and pay attention to it, the mind begins to loosen the hold it seems to have over us.

Another thing you'll notice as you observe the personalities of the mind is that some of them refer to you as "I". "I'm hungry. I want to get something to eat." And others say "You". "Why'd you say that? You always do that." When you hear any of the ones that call you "You" ask yourself, "Does that sound like someone from my past?"

If you are already aware of some thoughts that resurface from your past, note them here. Then ask yourself, do I really believe those thoughts?

_____

_____

_____

_____

_____

_____

_____

_____

_____

_____

I also discovered a truth of something else I'd read: the mind only lives in the past or the future. If the mind is thinking, it can only be thinking about something that's happened in the past; or speculating, maybe even worrying about something that hasn't happened yet, in the future. The mind is of no use in the present moment. If you think you can keep your mind fully present in a conversation, observe what happens. When the commentary is running, notice that it's speaking about what was just said. Maybe only a second or two behind, but the mind is still in the past. If the mind is telling you what to say next, it is in the future. The mind does not and cannot live in the present moment. Being in the present moment is about the experience. The mind doesn't experience, it evaluates the experience (past) or speculates about the experience (future).

Please don't just take my word for it, see for yourself by observing the mind in action.

When I first became consciously aware of my thoughts, another realization I had was regarding all the contradictions. One minute, I wasn't enough, the next it was telling me I was too good to put up with something. Which is it? "I'm not enough" or "I'm better than that"? I began to realize that how I felt about myself was dependent on what the mind decided to tell me at that moment. How silly is that?

I can't emphasize enough that this course is about observing the mind, not attempting to change it. Man's struggle with the mind has been going on for centuries. The nature of the mind is to think it is powerful enough to change itself. The mind's non-stop commentary has convinced us that our mind is who we are. The mind tells us we can change ourselves by changing it. Again, our mind is a wonderful tool, but we are so much more than this one tool. The third course is about seeing this tool for what it is and accepting it.

You will never fully understand these concepts until you *experience* them. You experience them by digesting this course and observing the mind.

"Seeing a thing once is better than hearing about it a hundred times."
-Chinese Proverb

Our mind has convinced us that it's in charge. We let it run our entire lives. You might be saying, "So what! I'd rather let my mind run my life than my big toe!" I agree with you on the big toe not being the best choice. However, don't you want to be in charge? So why not keep the mind in the toolbox until it's needed? Back to the analogy of your company Your Life and your mind is your board of directors. Even if your board is highly efficient and very organized, do you want them telling you how to feel about yourself? What if they pulled the file that said, "Remember second grade when you fell and everyone laughed at you? Well, I think that may happen again in today's meeting. This is a big meeting. You better not blow it because of your two left feet."

This is a great time to point out how the mind influences our emotions. The following chart demonstrates how the mind plays with our emotions.

"How little do they see what is, who frame their
judgments upon that which seems."
-Robert Southey (1774-1843)
English Poet

Fact	The Mind's Story	Emotional Response
What actually transpired?	About what it means	The response to the mind's story
Example #1	Two potential commentaries	Possible emotional responses
A man cuts you off in traffic	"What a rude, inconsiderate jerk! He could have killed me! Why don't people know how to drive?"	Anger. Frustration, etc.
	"I don't think he saw me. He looked like he was stressed. Maybe he's running late."	Compassion, understanding, etc.
Example #2:	Two potential commentaries	Two possible emotional responses
Your Boss speaks to you about a performance issue	"He's always on my back! He just watches and waits for me to mess up. He's just a bitter man who takes his misery out on me. I didn't do anything wrong."	Victimized, anger, etc
	"He's really trying to help me get better. He must really care about me and want to keep me as an employee; otherwise he'd just fire me."	Valuable, worthy, wanted, etc.

*"It isn't what you have, or who you are, or where you are,
or what you are doing that makes you happy or unhappy.
It's what you think about."*
-Dale Carnegie (1888-1955)
*American Author & Public Speaker known for Salesmanship,
Corporate Training & Interpersonal Skills*

The diagram illustrates that emotions don't arise directly in response to the **Facts** of a situation. If a guy cuts you off in traffic, it's nothing more than an experience. The story the mind tells you about that experience ignites the **Emotional Response** in you. **The Mind's Story** is what really ignites the emotion, not the experience.

"Suffering is not in the fact. Suffering is in the perception of the fact."
-Sri Bhagavan (Born 1949)
Spiritual Leader & Founder of Oneness University

"People are disturbed not by a thing, but by their perception of a thing."
-Epictetus (55-135) Greek Sage & Stoic Philosopher

The mind's stories create our perceptions. Those perceptions are responsible for our suffering. Since we resist suffering, we seek out distractions to avoid it. These distractions become our addictions. Not necessarily a substance addiction, but an addiction nonetheless. We will discuss this further in the next course of your meal.

*"I always felt like, I'll fight anybody. 'Cause everybody is the enemy,
the enemy, the enemy, the enemy, ya know. And now I'm here without
nothing, away from everyone, and I really took the time to find out, ya
know, who the enemy was. And it's not that it was the enemy; it was
the inna me; the inner me. Sometimes you realize
the true you is the enemy."*
-Kimbo Slice (Born 1974)
Bahamian-American Mixed Martial Arts Fighter

In the meantime, you may be perfectly comfortable letting the mind run the show. Might I suggest that you watch it for the entertainment value? It's certainly one of the best reality shows I've ever seen!

> *"The unexamined life is not worth living."*
> *-Socrates (469 BC—399 BC)*
> *Greek Philosopher*

Summary

1st Course **Accept that Ultimate Happiness Begins in the Inside World**

2nd Course **Accept ALL Feelings & Emotions**

3rd Course **Observe the Mind**

The 4th Course

When I was in Jr. High, my science teacher said, "Pain is a good thing." I remember thinking, "What is this guy on? Seriously, is he on drugs? Pain sucks!"

He went on to explain that pain is good because it serves as a signal that something is wrong. Like a fire alarm warns you so you can escape, pain signals you something needs attention. That lesson stayed with me for years. I began to think of pain as an alarm that was there for my benefit—to get my attention.

My teacher was correct; pain is a warning for us that something is going on beneath the surface. Although, if you take a look at the general direction Western healthcare has taken, it's pretty clear that most Americans share my initial mindset—pain sucks! We hate pain. We will do just about anything to avoid it. A friend recently told me that there are doctors who specialize in pain management. After further inquiry, I understand they write a lot of prescriptions. If we can take a pill and make it stop, why wouldn't we?

But why do we hate the alarm? We hate it so much we'll throw whatever we can at it to make it go away. If the alarm helps us, why do we go to such great lengths to avoid it?

If the alarm is there to serve as a warning that something is wrong beneath the surface, what happens if we silence it? Is everything beneath the surface better? If we turn off the fire alarm does the fire stop burning? Of course it doesn't.

If we look at pain in relation to the law of cause and effect, pain is an effect of some other cause. We have all become experts in the area of pain management; and not only as it relates to physical pain. The statistics in the first section revealed we are also medicating our emotional pain. And those figures don't even include self-medication options such as alcohol or illegal substances. According to The Huffington Post, American's spent $162 Billion on alcohol in 2011. Imagine what percentage of that is intended to sedate our internal pain.

Our pain management expertise doesn't just relate to medication and alcohol. We also use various distractions to take our mind off our pain. We use food, TV, work, video games, the internet, etc. We find things to do like organize/clean, see a movie, shop, play video games, call a friend, read, meditate, draw, play on social media, exercise, etc.

I'm not saying those things are bad for us, although some may find fault with a few of them. There are also a few items that can be very good for you like exercise or meditation. However, if used as a means to distract ourselves from the fire alarm, they could prevent us from escaping the fire.

Our biggest pain management tool is the mind. In the last course we discussed what a valuable tool the mind can be for us. Anything having to do with logic and reason, the mind is right for the job. But almost anyone can tell you that emotion has absolutely nothing to do with logic and reason. They are not even in the same realm. When you begin to see that the mind and its stories are actually responsible for our suffering, you'll recognize how ludicrous it is to expect the mind to solve what it's creating. It's like expecting a leak to fix itself.

"We can't solve problems by using the same kind of thinking we used when we created them."
-Albert Einstein (1879-1955)
Physicist & Philosopher, Nobel Prize in Physics (1921)

Again, the mind has convinced us we are it—it is us. Therefore, we hold the mind in very high regard. The mind values logic and reason and thinks emotions are a sign of weakness. This is prevalent in our culture. We can quickly become agitated when a child becomes emotional in public. I observed this on a flight recently. People became visibly irritated by a crying child. Some glared at the mother who wasn't *managing* the child's emotion. This is the cultural cage Dr. Scaer referred to on page 37.

Our culture values intelligence and emotion management. We respect someone who can remain calm in the face of crisis.

We look down at people who lose their temper, or cry in public or the workplace.

Ask your mind what you think of it. The mind will tell you just how great *you* think it is. The mind believes there is nothing it can't do. The mind loves itself and thrives on being in charge.

But there is something the mind can't do—process emotions. I mentioned in the second course, it actually inhibits the natural flow of emotions. It doesn't even understand emotions. It only understands categorizing, labeling, filing, logic, reason, etc. "Emotions are a waste of time—time that could be used for something far more valuable like thinking. Just stop having emotions, and think." What else would you expect the mind to say?

Again, the mind, with all its logic and judgments, interferes with our ability to experience emotions. In the second course you learned that we must experience emotions or we will end up carrying them around until we do. But our mind tells us how useless certain emotions are and how you are "better than that". It says, "You aren't afraid. You're a strong person for crying out loud. Don't be a wimp." Or, "You don't have time to be angry about that jerk. He's not worth it. Shake it off."

Let's look at how the mind attempts to manage our emotions. Let's say you have a disagreement with someone in your family or significant other. You begin to feel angry. What does the mind do? Take notice of the judgments the mind makes in this process.

- First it plays the situation over and over again. It's like an insane video player that keeps playing, rewinding, playing, rewinding, etc. All the while it is resisting what happened, saying things like, "She shouldn't have said that, I should've told him this, she's unreasonable, he's a jerk, etc." It looks something like this:

The mind keeps taking you back to its story; convinced that the story is the key to being free from our emotional pain. The story does not free us from the emotion, it perpetuates it. It caused the emotion in the first place and then perpetuates it. Not only does this loop not lead to our freedom, it actually imprisons us.

> *"The mind is a great problem solver. Unfortunately,*
> *it is an equally great problem creator."*
> *-Stuart Mooney, Jr. (Born 1948)*
> *American Author & Spiritual Teacher*

- Even after you leave the situation, the mind keeps playing and rewinding what happened (living in the past). As it does, it continues to compile data on why you were right and the other person was wrong. This is always the mind's story. Translation: blame, blame, blame. Even if you leave the room or the situation, your mind doesn't stop blaming. You'd think blaming the other person for everything, leaving you responsible for nothing, would make you feel better. But it doesn't.
- So, it moves on to logic and reason to try to bring you back from this unproductive emotion. After all, you are a level-headed individual. So, you try to understand why the disagreement happened. The mind may come up with some real or imagined reason it happened. This may work in stopping the emotion, but it probably won't. When it doesn't, you may go on to look for some deeper meaning. After all, "everything happens for a reason" right?
- When nothing else has worked, the mind may tell you, "Snap out of this. This isn't doing anything for you." Or "you need to find something better to do." You will then choose some suitable distraction—you'll eat, drink, meditate, exercise, watch TV, commiserate by calling a friend to discuss the situation and gain support regarding how right you are, work, etc. All as a means to escape the pain, anger in this case.

When we leave our mind in charge of our emotional pain management, we are prevented from effectively *experiencing* the emotion. Remember, the mind lives in the past or future and the experience is in the present moment.

Besides being a nuisance to the mind, what is an emotion anyway? The easiest explanation to understand is that it's energy in motion (e-motion). Lightning is also energy in motion. Expecting the mind to handle an emotion is like trying to grab a lightning bolt with your hand. If you did that you'd be in far more pain, right?

"Simply put, emotions are the feedback devices through which the energy body communicates with the conscious mind, just as physical pain is the feedback device through which the physical body communicates with the conscious mind about its states of being."
-Dr. Silvia Hartmann (Born 1959) German Author

We also discussed in the second course that every human being has been faced with negative emotions. If you are still fighting this, you are only making your pain stronger. Remember? What you resist persists. Physics scientifically proves this. You may recall this one from school: for every action there is an equal and opposite reaction. The more you push, the more it pushes back.

In other words, when the mind practices emotional pain management, it creates more pain. And the funny thing about pain, if you don't listen to the alarm it will try another route to get your attention. Next time it may not be a negative emotion, it may be a dis-ease kind of pain. Any medical professional will tell you emotional pain like stress can turn into a physical illness.

Bottom line of what we've covered so far:
- Pain, both emotional and physical, is an alarm
- Pain, emotional and physical, is an effect of a deeper cause
- If our mind has labeled an emotion painful, it will attempt to manage it by silencing it
- When silenced, the cause will send a different kind of alarm in an attempt to get your attention

So what do we do?

Begin by considering another analogy. I believe that the soul is here to visit an amusement park called "Life". The soul wants to go on all the rides to *experience* everything. It wants to go on the rides that make you exhilarated, the ones that scare the heck out of you, the romantic rides and of course the "Fun House"! Recognize that the soul loves all of them, even if the mind wishes to avoid some like the plague. Again, the soul wants to experience everything, even the emotions that the mind desperately wants us to avoid. Our freedom from emotions lies in the experience.

"Anything fully experienced turns to joy."
-Sri Bhagavan (Born 1949)
Spiritual Leader & Founder of Oneness University

In the second course I pointed out the contradiction between accepting and experiencing emotions in some teachings, when other teachings encourage us to focus on changing negative emotions to positive. Now that we know how our magic bow & arrow works, it makes sense that we would want to use it to our advantage. So the mind says, "I should focus on things that I want and feel all the positive emotions that will serve as the fuel or power to get me there." Makes sense, right? We also know that all we have to do is experience an emotion to be free from it.

So, what happens the next time we have a negative emotion after someone treats us in a way we think is unfair? Do we feel it, experience it, allow it, etc.? But if we do that, won't we be attracting more negativity by feeling a negative feeling? Or do we grab the bow & arrow, aim at something else and try to make ourselves feel happy about it?

Let's discuss what it means to *fully experience* an emotion. Does it mean to scream, yell, curse, blame and throw or hit things to experience anger? Again, those things are outside world options and our true power comes from the inside world. Does experiencing an emotion mean to think about it since thinking is an inside world option? Nope. We learned earlier that logic actually interferes with our ability to experience an emotion.

This, I believe, is the key to understanding the contradiction. The bow & arrow uses both the mind and our emotions. If you fully experience an emotion in the present moment, the mind is not engaged at all. If you are not thinking, you are not aiming at anything. You are merely releasing energy in motion. Imagine your bow & arrow sitting next to you while your arm is just moving back and forth. The arrow is going nowhere. When the negative energy is gone, you can pick up the bow & arrow and consciously aim at something positive, while feeling positive. Thus, you will attract more positive experiences.

Experiencing means to *feel* the emotion and let it pass through us, having nothing to do with the person who wronged us or the situation that triggered the feeling in the first place. This sounds so easy doesn't it? It is easy; the hard part is getting the mind to step aside and let it happen. We've let the mind run the show for so long that it's a bit of a challenge to get it to let someone else do the job. Your mind is like the hand that swears it can catch the lightning bolt. Using logic and reason, the mind will give you plenty of data to support how effective it's been in managing your emotions up until now. I don't know how else to say this, so I'll be direct—it's lying to you. It has been sweeping so many emotions under the rug; all of which we are carrying around. And it's costing us a fortune! Billions of dollars in health problems that aren't accounted for in the figures mentioned earlier. Plus, it's robbing us of our chance for ultimate happiness.

The only way to get ourselves out of this mess that pain management has created is to *experience* emotions as they come and begin to clean out the ones the mind has been busy sweeping under the rug.

How do we do that?

"Beneath every emotion lies bliss."
-*Unknown*

The best way I can describe this is to ask you to think of your feelings in layers. Initially you may feel angry when someone has treated you poorly. If you fully experience the anger, you will then find you are hurt by what this treatment means to you. If you stay with the hurt, it will pass. Then you'll come to the fear. You may be thinking, fear of what? After all, you were angry, what does that have to do with fear? At the core, we are usually afraid of not being enough or that we aren't worthy of love. If you fully experience the fear, what comes next is bliss. But to get to the freedom of bliss you have to walk through the other emotions to get there.

> *"The only way out is through."*
> -Robert Frost (1874-1963)
> *American Poet & recipient of 4 Pulitzer Prizes for Poetry*

Have you ever noticed that the human body is designed to *experience* all of life? The body allows us to smell, to see, to touch, to hear, to taste and to feel. That's right; the body is far more qualified to experience emotions than the mind will ever be. This leads us to your fourth course.

Observe the Body

The next time you feel an uncomfortable emotion, bring your attention to how it feels in your body. After all, an emotion is energy in motion. So spend some time paying attention to how that energy affects your body. How does it affect your breathing? Is it fast or slow? Deep or shallow? Does your heart beat fast or slow? Gentle or pounding? You may feel some tension in your body where energy is accumulating. Can you find the emotional energy collecting anywhere in your body? In your neck? Your shoulders? In your hands/fists? Is it in your stomach? How about the back of your throat?

Bringing your focus to the body helps to disengage the mind from its desire to *help*. In other words, put the bow & arrow down. Stay present, by focusing on the body. This allows the emotion to flow through without resistance.

The mind will not be comfortable sitting this one out. At first the mind may report on the body's state. Almost certainly, it will continue to try to get involved in the story (blame, reason, assign a deeper meaning or choose a suitable distraction option) assuring you that it can help you feel better. The goal here is for the energy to pass and then you will feel better. So, when you catch yourself thinking, bring your focus back to the body until you can feel the energy pass through you.

Another approach that seemed to be effective for me was to treat the negative emotion like it's a crying infant who has no logic or reasoning abilities. Tell your mind, logic and reason won't help here. All you can do is pick up the baby and hold it until the emotion passes. No judging how stupid it is. No telling him/her that this is such a waste of time. Just hold it until it passes. No logic, no reason, no opinions and no beliefs.

After you begin to allow negative emotions, you will likely begin to notice there are some emotions you experience more than others. The frequent emotions are a pretty good indicator of where our past emotional baggage lies. The mind may have a desire to revisit your childhood to discover where this frequent emotion may have first begun. There may be some value for you in this or there may not. Exploring some of my childhood memories helped me learn some interesting things about myself. At a certain point I knew I'd gotten enough from looking at the past. I came to believe that if it's important for me to *know* something specific, the memory will come to me. I don't have to go digging for it.

Please be aware, as you begin to allow some of this past emotional baggage out, it may feel like your life is getting worse. Your mind may say, "You are supposed to be feeling better, but you keep feeling these negative emotions. Your back hurts and your outside world is getting worse!" Things may seem worse as stored emotions surface and are released through your experience of them. I like to think of it as lightening our load along our journey towards ultimate happiness. Your life will soon be back on target wherever you consciously aim and fire your magic bow & arrow!

When I first began to feel some of these stored negative emotions, I was amazed how the mind really looked for any means of distracting me from the energy associated with my physical or emotional pain. It was always suggesting escape routes—things I could do rather than sit still and physically experience anything. The mind would say, "Why don't you make that phone call? Hey, you haven't eaten in a while, shouldn't you eat? And what about all the email you have? I have so much to do, how can I justify just sitting here?" I chose to ignore the thoughts and focus on the body for 1-10 minutes. Once I consciously felt the emotions as energy, the process was far easier and faster than the mental alternative. I realized how exhausting the crazy video player and mental analysis can be. I trust you will find the same, should you choose to ignore the thoughts and *experience* the feeling by observing the body.

Just like any skill, it won't be easy at first. However, with practice you can master this. If you pay attention you will physically feel the energy leave your body. Once you stop resisting and begin allowing, your whole life will begin to flow with greater ease.

"We must consciously feel what is out of balance to restore the balance. In other words, we must feel it to heal it."
-Michael Brown (Born 1962)
South African Author

"To end suffering, suffer."
-Sri Bhagavan (Born 1949)
Spiritual Leader & Founder of Oneness University

Once you've observed the body as it experiences negative emotions, you may want to try the other versions of this course.
• Observe the body as it experiences positive emotions
• Be aware of your body and how it moves
• Observe breath
• Observe posture
• Focus on physical pain/discomfort
• Observe the body at rest
• Pay attention to how your body responds to different stimuli; notice how it's affected by different foods, caffeine, nicotine, alcohol, etc. How does it feel when you watch TV or listen to the news?
• Observe how it feels to be alive inside the body

The more you place your focus on your body, the easier it will become. Your mind will also come to really appreciate the break.

Let's try it right now. Please read the following suggestions before you begin:
• You may want to scan the questions several times. Don't worry if you can't remember all of them. You'll get the idea, so feel free to improvise with your own questions.
• Close your eyes.
• Bring your attention to your breath. Don't try to change it.

Just observe how you breathe. Is it shallow or deep? Do you breathe through your nose or mouth? Into your chest or belly?

- Observe how it feels to be alive.
- Place your focus on your feet. Without moving them, focus on how they feel.
- Slowly shift your focus to your calves. Once you really feel them, shift your focus to your thighs. Then your torso. Can you feel your heartbeat? Can you feel it in different parts of your body?
- Continue slowly moving your focus to your hands, lower arms, upper arms and neck, until you reach your head.
- Notice what you see when your eyes are closed. Is it black? If you keep your focus there, do you begin to see static? Or colors?
- Do you feel any sensations in the body? Twitches, tingles, swallowing or discomfort?
- How does your body experience *life*?

What does it mean to experience an emotion? How do I do it?

_____

_____

_____

_____

_____

_____

_____

What does it mean to observe my body?

_____

_____

_____

_____

_____

_____

<u>Summary</u>

1st Course	**Accept that Ultimate Happiness Begins in the Inside World**
2nd Course	**Accept ALL Feelings & Emotions**
3rd Course	**Observe the Mind**
4th Course	**Observe the Body**

The 5th Course

This course is a piece of cake (pun intended) once you've fully digested and experienced the first four courses. This course gave me a whole new meaning for the saying, "You must first be able to love yourself, before you can truly love another." It's true. If I do not accept myself completely, exactly as I am, including what the mind has labeled flaws, how on earth will I ever be able to accept another with all of their flaws?

As you experience the first four courses, you'll begin to notice you're judging yourself less and accepting yourself more. You will become comfortable in the observer role and that makes this course easier.

Observe as you begin to Accept Others Unconditionally

In other words, mastery of the first four courses makes this one part of a natural progression. Once you've mastered observing and accepting yourself without judgment, you will begin to observe and accept others in all sorts of situations.

> *"He who falls in love with himself will have no rivals."*
> *-Benjamin Franklin (1706-1790)*
> *One of the Founding Fathers of the United States,*
> *Politician, Scientist & Inventor*

Since practicing precedes mastery, or experiencing precedes being, I can offer a few strategies that may help as you dine on this course.

Review the first four courses and continually practice *experiencing* them. Remember this meal's goal is for you to develop the skills to experience ultimate happiness. Skills take practice, not just knowledge and understanding.

You'll judge. By now, you may have begun to accept that the mind is judgmental. If not, just remember the only way to stop judging is to lose your mind. If you observe yourself making judgments about others, you can ask the mind to re-mind you of a time when you behaved similarly to the person you are judging. You'll soon realize we do, or used to do, the very things that annoy us most.

> *"Let him who is without sin cast the first stone."*
> *-John 8:7*

The more you practice sitting in the observer role, the more you will notice a whole lot of silly things we humans do.

Note that this course says *accept*. Think of it as accepting *what is*. That doesn't mean you need to love, love, love everything.

> *"Instead of loving your enemies,*
> *treat your friends a little better."*
> *-Ed Howe (1853-1937)*
> *American Writer & Newspaper & Magazine Editor*

How would you feel about trying to accept something that opposed your deepest beliefs? For most of us, changing our deepest beliefs seems next to impossible. Instead of trying to accept something you don't believe, begin by accepting that you will cross paths with people who have beliefs opposing yours.

> *"Hate the sin, love the sinner."*
> *-Mahatma Gandhi (1869-1948)*
> *Political & Spiritual Leader of India*

Again, this is not about changing people—changing them to fit how your mind tells you they should be. This is about accepting them exactly as they are, including their flaws.

"Everyone thinks of changing the world, but
no one thinks of changing himself."
-*Count Leo Tolstoy (1828-1910)*
Russian Nobility & Author of "War and Peace"

Again, if you're not bothered that the sun rises in the east, why be bothered when you encounter a human being doing, thinking or feeling something your mind says is *wrong*, within reason? I'm no psychic, but I feel confident in making the following statements:
1. You are going to behave in ways that oppose the beliefs of others.
2. Others are going to behave in ways that oppose your beliefs.
3. You are even going to behave in ways that oppose your own beliefs, usually provided the mind believes the circumstances make it ok. The mind will provide justification that your violation of your "rules" is totally warranted.

The last one may take an example to illustrate. Let's assume you believe stealing is wrong and you say, "I would *never* steal." If your child was dying and you didn't have the medicine that would cure him/her and you see someone had left a hundred doses of the cure on their front porch, you might feel the circumstances make it ok for you to take a dose to save your child's life. The mind might say, "It's only one dose; they have a hundred. Besides, they left them unattended, so they must not care. They probably won't even notice." Or, "I'd kill to save my child's life, stealing is nothing."

Interesting how our mind can offer justification when we wish to violate one of our own beliefs. The mind will make the story fit any action it wants to. Watch how often you do this, even in cases far less extreme than the life or death example.

Have you ever noticed people doing the very thing they complain about or swear they would *never* do? Like a friend or family member who cuts people off in traffic all the time then has a temper tantrum when someone cuts them off. If you point this out to them, watch how the mind justifies why it's ok for them to do it, but not the other person. Sometimes they will even blame you for the very thing they are doing. They'll yell, "Why are you always yelling at me?!"

As you practice the first four courses, you will begin to accept that we all violate the mind's beliefs, those of others and even our own. And the mind will always justify the violations. If you accept that this is how the mind operates, you will begin to accept it in others. The mind may take some time to come around, but if you're patient it will come to accept its own flip-flopping. Until then, feel free to borrow one of my light hearted responses to the question, "Do you really like everyone?"

"I love everyone. It's just that the mind finds
fault with the mind in others."
Student of Life, Servant, Author & Storyteller

Besides, have you ever tried to change a human being who wasn't ready to change? I'll admit I have—frustrating task, right? It takes huge amounts of effort with very minimal results; in other words, horrible return on investment (ROI). Personally, I think it has to do with the "what you resist persists" theory. Interestingly, I saw far greater results after giving up on changing another. Once I accepted that all my efforts were hopeless, they changed. It must have something to do with *accepting*.

Summary

1st Course **Accept that Ultimate Happiness Begins in the Inside World**
2nd Course **Accept ALL Feelings & Emotions**
3rd Course **Observe the Mind**
4th Course **Observe the Body**
5th Course **Observe as you begin to Accept Others Unconditionally**

The 6ᵗʰ Course

I've always loved mentally challenging conversations. As a teen, I remember challenging my friends, "Giving is not a selfless act." They would argue that it is possible to give without thinking of themselves. But they could never get around one point—how good it feels when we do something nice for someone without expecting anything in return.

"It is one of the beautiful compensations of this life that no one can sincerely try to help another without helping himself."
-Ralph Waldo Emerson (1803-1882)
American Philosopher & Poet

It feels good. No one can deny it. Think about the last time you went out of your way to help someone in need. Take a moment to remember the situation. Remember it as vividly as you possibly can. What was the day like? What happened that caused you to help? What did you do? What were your thoughts before you decided to help? After helping this person, how did you feel?

_____

_____

_____

_____

_____

_____

_____

_____

The fact is we cannot give without receiving. When we give without obligation or without expecting something in return, at a minimum we receive a good feeling.

"For it is in giving that we receive."
-St. Francis (1181-1226)
Catholic Deacon & Patron Saint of Animals & the Environment

If you look at this from the Oneness teachings, when we give, we are giving to our self, the One. Scientifically speaking, there is part of the brain that doesn't know if we are giving or receiving.

In a film called The Moses Code, author and psychologist Harville Henrix explains it this way, "There is a part of the limbic brain that is not time or object oriented. Meaning, it can't tell the difference between itself and others. And it has no sense of past, present or future. That timeless and objectless place in my brain receives when I'm giving because it doesn't know whether it's going out or coming in. So, if you criticize other people, your brain doesn't know you're criticizing them. It receives it as if it was self-directed. If you care for and give to another person, that part of the brain doesn't know which way it's going, so it always receives. The brain always receives as a gift to itself what is given to another person."

That means the way you treat others, is how this part of your brain perceives you're treating YOU. That gave me a whole new meaning to the old adage, "When you point a finger at someone else there are 3 pointing back at you."

Whether you look at the teachings or your own personal experience, giving and receiving are closely linked. By now you've probably concluded that this course is made up of two ingredients.

Give and Receive

While these ingredients are equally enjoyable alone, when balance is achieved, the combination is magical.

"To receive everything, one must open his hands and give."
-Taisen Deshimaru (1914-1982)
Japanese Soto Zen Buddhist

Not only do you receive when you give, it also works the other way around. When you receive, you also give. I'll give you a minute for the mind to digest that one. After all, most of us were taught that giving is good. Where receiving is not necessarily bad, some perceive it demonstrates a lack of something. We aren't always comfortable with others thinking we lack anything, because that would be like exposing our "not enough" button. Those who are attached to that kind of belief will go to great lengths to become the best givers, in an effort to prove they are enough.

Let me share a simple example of how receiving is also an act of giving. I'll assume at some point in your life you've had the opportunity to buy a meal for someone. When the waiter brings the check you say, "Let me get that," or, "It's on me." Think back to the first time you did that. Maybe you'd received your first paycheck, or a big bonus and you wanted to celebrate and share the moment with another. How did you feel? You gave and received, right? You gave the meal and received a really great feeling. So, let's flip it. Imagine you are out with someone who says, "I got it." By receiving, with a side of gratitude, you are giving the other person a chance to receive the great feelings that come from giving to you.

Again, we are talking about the concept of balance. Or, you can choose to look at giving and receiving as part of some sort of circular cause and effect relationship.

> *"You can have everything in life that you want if you just give enough other people what they want."*
> *-Zig Ziglar (Born 1926)*
> *American Author & Motivational Speaker*

For this course I would highly encourage you to observe your giving/receiving ratio. Is there balance? Is there a lack of balance? What are the effects of any imbalance? Are you interested in finding balance?

_____

_____

_____

_____

If you find you have a give/receive ratio that is out of balance and you want to find balance, do it! Sounds easy right?

Chronic Giver

If you are a chronic giver you may be so busy giving that you are thinking, "Ya right, when am I going to find the time to receive, I'm too busy taking care of everyone and everything else!" Or, "Who is going to give to me? I'm surrounded by people who need me. They can't take care of themselves, how are they going to take care of me?"

The solution is simple. Put yourself on the list! You know, the list of everyone you need to give to. I'd suggest that you put YOU pretty close to the top of the list. I'll go back to the airplane oxygen mask example. You cannot help another effectively without helping yourself first. If you take care of you, you are better equipped to give to others.

I'll share what helped me change my paradigm. I spent a good amount of time as a chronic giver. I still do at times, for that matter. It began soon after I decided I would no longer be selfish (this was long before I'd ever tasted our second course and learned that denying a part of who we are is an unproductive task for most human beings). Anyway, after *resolving* my perceived character flaw of selfishness, I was determined to prove my success by giving. I gave and gave and gave. Yet when I needed help, no one was around for me. This caused me some frustration. After all, what about all my good karma? What goes around comes around? That was not my experience. You see, I invested so much in the belief that I didn't need anyone or anything. Not only had I come to believe it, but everyone else around me bought into too.

After digesting our second course, I practiced embracing my selfishness and accepted that I needed TLC too. Once I was able to do that, I put my selfish little self on the list of those I wanted to give to. I choose to look at it this way: she's my inner child and thinks I'm her parent. If I blow her off, she is going to be affected just the way a child would be impacted by an inattentive parent—a parent who was too busy giving to everyone else. I got tired of telling my inner child that everyone else was more important than her.

As I began to give to myself from this mindset, I came to experience something else that's referenced in many teachings. No one can love my inner child better than I can.

> *"No one saves us but ourselves. No one can and no one may. We ourselves must walk the path."*
> *-Buddha (563BCE—483 BCE)*
> *Spiritual Teacher*

All the while, most of us look to others to show us how loved we are. Now I think of it this way: if I wait for someone else to show my inner child how loved she is, I liken it to dropping her off at the babysitter and telling her, "Listen honey, Mommy's really busy. So, the baby sitter is going to tell you how much you are loved."

If I pay a little attention to her, she is happy and feels loved. She then helps me find more peace in my life, along with the energy to give to others.

In all seriousness, how loving a parent are you to your inner child? Who have you been relying on to make sure he/she feels loved?

_____

_____

_____

_____

_____

_____

_____

If you start to make this paradigm shift, it will really become clear that you need you, far more than you need others to take care of you. *You* need to take care of you!

Chronic Receiver

If you grew up in an environment of lack or scarcity, you may find it difficult to give. Since I grew up financially poor compared to my peers, I had this one too. Frankly, I think this led to my being so selfish in the first place!

If this has been your experience, you likely have an underlying fear of being without something. The thought may be, "How can I give to someone else when I feel like I don't have enough for myself?"

My suggestion is to begin giving from a place where you are abundant. For example, let's say you are like many Americans who are living paycheck to paycheck. You may not feel comfortable making a financial contribution to a charity at this point. But, there are millions of other ways to give that wouldn't cost you a dime.

> *"Nobody made a greater mistake than he who did*
> *nothing because he could do only a little."*
> *-Edmund Burke (1729-1797)*
> *Irish Statesman who served in Britain's House of Commons,*
> *Author & Philosopher*

> *"If you have much, give of your wealth. If you*
> *have little, give of your heart."*
> *-Arabian Proverb*

If you do give of your wealth, I suggest you observe how you feel in your body, as you write the check or make that contribution.

If you are not wealthy, I'll bet you can find abundance in your life to give any one of the following:
- A genuine smile
- Call a friend just to say "thanks for being in my life"
- A sincere "thank you" to someone who provided you with good service at a local business
- When you are not in a rush, let someone go ahead of you in line

> *"Never worry about numbers. Help one person at a time,*
> *and always start with the person nearest you."*
> *-Mother Teresa (1910-1997)*
> *Albanian Catholic Nun*

- Volunteer for an hour at a charity that you will feel good about

- Ask an elderly person to share one of their favorite moments in life
- Make a homemade gift or card for someone you care about
- Compliment people at work for recent contributions
- Listen intently to a friend's problem

You can't do anything without receiving a gift that is far greater. In other words, the return on investment is exceptional.

"The best thing about giving of ourselves is that what we get is always better than what we give. The reaction is greater than the action."
-Orison Swett Marden, M.D. (1850-1924)
American Writer, Harvard Medical Graduate
& Successful Hotel Owner

The return on your investment is often a feeling, which can't be quantified—probably another reason the mind doesn't see the value in feelings or emotions. But when you pay attention to that feeling, you will recognize this course of your meal has you beginning to feel *full*.

"You make a living by what you get. You make a life by what you give."
-Winston Churchill (1874-1965)
British Prime Minister & regarded as a Great Wartime Leader

Summary

1st Course	**Accept that Ultimate Happiness Begins in the Inside World**
2nd Course	**Accept ALL Feelings & Emotions**
3rd Course	**Observe the Mind**
4th Course	**Observe the Body**
5th Course	**Observe as you begin to Accept Others Unconditionally**
6th Course	**Give and Receive**

The 7ᵗʰ Course

Now it is time for dessert. Virtually every teaching on the subject of happiness speaks to the importance of gratitude.

> *"In daily life we must see that it is not happiness that makes us grateful. But gratefulness that makes us happy."*
> *-David Steindl Rast (Born 1926)*
> *Austrian-American Roman Catholic Theologian*

> *"All happy people are grateful. Ungrateful people cannot be happy. We tend to think that being unhappy leads people to complain, but it's truer to say that complaining leads to people becoming unhappy."*
> *-Dennis Prager (Born 1948)*
> *American Syndicated Radio Host & Syndicated Columnist*

This course will satisfy a hunger in you that cannot fully be described—it must be *experienced*.

Spend Time Daily Feeling Grateful

How does gratitude bring more happiness into your life? Explanations vary, based on the teaching. Again, the law of attraction operates from the principal of physics where thoughts and emotions have an energetic vibration. Therefore, if you are thinking and feeling gratitude, you attract things to be grateful for. This isn't something you can fake. At least I haven't mastered how to fake the exact same energetic vibration for gratitude. You must actually *feel* grateful. So, how do you get yourself to feel grateful? Remember the mind can ignite emotions. So, use it to your benefit. Think of what you are grateful for until you begin to feel it in your body.

> *"A grateful mind is a great mind which eventually*
> *attracts to itself great things."*
> *-Plato (428/7 BC-348/7 BC)*
> *Greek Mathematician & Philosopher*

Spiritual and religious teachings point to the importance of gratitude relating to prayer.

> *"If the only prayer you said in your whole life*
> *was 'thank you' that would suffice."*
> *-Meister Eckhardt (1260-1327)*
> *German Theologian & Philosopher*

If you have faith that your Higher Power answers all prayers, once you make a prayer request, you would immediately feel grateful. Grateful, because your faith would give you a knowing that your prayer has been heard and is already answered. In other words, it's on its way.

When you go to a restaurant, what do you do after the waitress takes your order? Do you sit back, relax and enjoy the people you are with until the food arrives? Do you believe, or have faith, that she will bring your order? Or do you sit there and worry? "I ordered a grilled cheese; I hope she brings me a grilled cheese. I wonder if I was clear. Maybe I should ask her again in a nicer voice. What if she doesn't think I deserve a grilled cheese?" Do you stop her every time she passes you and say, "Please, please, please bring me a grilled cheese. If you bring me a grilled cheese, I promise to be a better person." This is how some people pray.

If we continue to pray over and over for the same thing, we demonstrate that we're not sure our prayer was even heard, or that we have the faith that it will be answered. So, does that mean we have more faith in our waitress than our Higher Power? Feeling grateful for our prayer request demonstrates our faith that it is already being answered. Feeling grateful demonstrates faith. Now, if you believe your Higher Power knows all, won't It also know if you have faith and are truly grateful? Again, gratitude can't be faked.

It really doesn't matter which school of thought you subscribe to. Either way, to *experience* gratitude you must *feel* it.

If you are reading this and having a tough time finding reasons to be grateful, odds are you have been stuffing yourself with all sorts of things in an attempt to satisfy your hunger for happiness. Only to find that no matter how hard you try, you're still hungry for more. Remember Maslow? It's really difficult to be grateful for what you just ate if you're still hungry. When you're hungry, you're already thinking about your next meal.

> *"The hardest arithmetic to master is that which*
> *enables us to count our blessings."*
> *-Eric Hoffer (1902-1983)*
> *American Writer & Philosopher*

If you are feeling challenged by this, the easiest way I know to find gratitude is to change your perspective. Right now your life may not be satisfying, because you are immersed in it. It is overwhelming—the only thing you can see. Changing your perspective allows you to see your life from another view.

This should help you look at your life from another perspective. I got this in an email called the Global Village.

Global Village

If you could fit the entire population of the world into a village consisting of 100 people maintaining the proportions of all the people living on Earth, that village would consist of:
- 57 Asians
- 21 Europeans
- 14 Americans (North, Central and South)
- 8 Africans

There would be:
- 52 women and 48 men
- 30 Caucasians and 70 non-Caucasians
- 30 Christians and 70 non-Christians
- 89 heterosexuals
- 11 homosexuals

6 people would possess 59% of the wealth and they would ALL come from the USA

- 80 would live in poverty
- 70 would be illiterate
- 50 would suffer from hunger and malnutrition
- 1 would be dying
- 1 would be being born
- 1 would own a computer
- 1 would have a college degree

Consider the following:

- If you woke up this morning in good health, you have more luck than one million people, who won't live through the week
- If you have never experienced the horror of war, the solitude of prison, the pain of torture, being close to death from starvation, you are better off than 500 million people
- If you can go to your place of worship without fearing someone will assault or kill you, then you are luckier than 3 billion people
- If you have a full fridge, clothes on your back, a roof over your head and a warm place to sleep, you are wealthier than 75% of the world's population
- If you currently have money in the bank, in your wallet and a few coins in your purse, you are one of the 8 privileged people in your village.

Whether the statistics are correct or not is irrelevant. The question is: did looking at your life from a different perspective make you feel differently? Are you feeling more grateful? How does it feel in your body? What is the mind saying? Is it telling you how lucky you really are? Or are you hearing a lecture, "Did you hear that? You are wealthier than 75% of the world's population and you're always saying how broke you are!"

_____

_____

_____

_____

_____

_____

_____

"Let us rise up and be thankful, for if we didn't learn a lot today, at least we learned a little, and if we didn't learn a little, at least we didn't get sick, and if we got sick, at least we didn't die; so, let us all be thankful."
-Buddha (563BCE-483 BCE)
Spiritual Teacher

If changing your perspective didn't fill you with gratitude, you may want to spend some time thinking about any of the following to get the feelings of gratitude flowing:
- Someone you love
- Friends or family
- A pet
- Your favorite song
- Your material things
- The best moment in your life
- The last time you laughed so hard your cheeks and belly ached
- Your talents or skills—your gifts
- A movie that touched your heart
- The cutest thing you've heard a child say

It doesn't matter what it takes to cause you to feel grateful, the point is that you *feel* it.

"Gratitude is the fairest blossom which springs from the soul."
-Henry Ward Beecher (1813-1887)
American Congregational Minister

Once you find something that you are grateful for, really paint a picture of it. Take yourself to it. This will help to intensify the feeling. Some people are visual so they understand when I say "paint a picture." For others, sound may be more important. Tell yourself the story of a moment you were grateful, or take yourself to a time of gratitude with the help of a song, or other sounds. Other people need to move to feel it. So dance and move your body like it's grateful. Jump up and down like you just got the best news of your life. If you're not sure what's going to help intensify your feelings, try them all. And if the mind tells you how silly this is . . . ignore it!

If you spend time every day feeling grateful, I promise your life, and your experience of it, will improve in ways you can't yet imagine.

Bottom line: the ROI for this course is off the charts!

"Gratitude is not only the greatest
of virtues, but the parent of all others."
-Marcus Cicero (106 BC—43 BC)
Roman Lawyer, Statesman & Philosopher

Consuming this seven course meal in your daily life will satisfy the hunger of your soul. You will be able to lead a life that is full. You will no longer feel compelled to run the impossible race of the outside world. You can still choose to play in the outside world, but you will do it with a greater wisdom. You will know exactly what will fill you up and what will taste good for a moment but leave you feeling hungry. You can continue to eat both, but you will know the difference.

Many will continue to suffer as they starve, looking for a filling meal in the outside world. Not you. You'll have the freedom to choose whatever you want, fast food in the outside world, or a meal you know will satisfy the hunger of the soul in the inside world. Your soul will be free—free to feel full whenever it wants!

Your soul's freedom is a result of *experiencing* this meal.

Summary

1st Course **Accept that Ultimate Happiness Begins in the Inside World**
2nd Course **Accept ALL Feelings & Emotions**
3rd Course **Observe the Mind**
4th Course **Observe the Body**
5th Course **Observe as you begin to Accept Others Unconditionally**
6th Course **Give and Receive**
7th Course **Spend Time Daily Feeling Grateful**

Part 3

Experiencing
the Meal

Flavor Enhancers

Recommended by Your Maître d'

I'm not a big wine drinker, but there are plenty of people who believe wine is an integral part of a good meal. Integral, not only because it enhances the flavors, but some data even points to health benefits, including digestion. Others prefer the use of herbs and spices for flavor enhancement.

In this section, I'd like to share a couple of things that made this meal more enjoyable for me. They also made it easier to digest, especially as I transitioned from *knowing* what I'd learned, to *experiencing* it.

Everything in this section comes merely from my perspective and my experiences. Although, if you were to compare these flavor enhancers to condiments, I'd say they are like salt and pepper because they seem pretty basic and appeal to most palates/tastes. I haven't come across anyone who has shared a harsh reaction to any of the following suggestions.

However, I don't want to allude that anyone's experience will be like mine. Nor would I ever want to tell anyone what to believe. The inside world has all the answers for you. I do not propose that my outside world stories should alter your beliefs in any way. However, I do want to share what I believe made for a tastier experience, hoping it may help others more easily digest this meal.

For that reason, I am going to share my three favorite flavor enhancers:

- Breath Awareness
- Meditation
- Yoga

Breath Awareness

Take a deep breath and let it out with a sigh. Aren't you relieved you already know how to do this one? I'm certain you're good enough at breathing that you don't even have to think about it. Paying focused attention to your breath is what breath awareness is all about.

Many teachings draw an important connection between our breath and spirit, as it gives us life. Personally, I found significant changes in my perspective after I began to pay attention to my breath. I began spending fifteen minutes, twice a day, observing and consciously connecting my breath. Some people have experiences during breath awareness like moments of unexplained emotion or various physical sensations, even slight discomfort. For me nothing too exciting happened during my breathing sessions. However, I did notice some pretty interesting changes in my day to day life. I began to see the situations in my life from a different view.

Think of a tapestry, or a rug with a pattern. When you are super close, you can see each stitch. Back up a little and you can see a section. When you step back further, you can see a whole design. When you are able to step back from your life and see it from another perspective, you begin to see the patterns. In my experience, paying attention to my breath helped in elevating my consciousness, or my perspective.

There are many books and teachings about consciousness. In a nutshell, consciousness is your perspective—your viewpoint—your outlook on life. I think of it like a mountain. Where I am on the mountain determines my view or my outlook in life. As you move up the mountain you can see more. In the same way, as your consciousness moves up, you see life from a completely different viewpoint. I think most consciousness experts would agree with me when I say there is a direct correlation between consciousness and happiness. So, elevating your consciousness elevates your happiness. Want to be happier? Put effort toward things or practices that aid in elevating consciousness, like breath awareness.

The most challenging thing about practicing breath awareness is that your mind thinks it's a completely useless task. It may say, "If I can breathe without thinking about it, why should I focus on it? There is no way that paying attention to your breathing is going to give you a different perspective on your life. I don't care what this woman says; there are far more important things for me to think about and you want me to watch you breathe?"

The mind expresses its concern to me often. "How on earth does paying attention to my breath change my outlook in life?" I do know it has, but I don't know how. This is another time when I remind myself that I don't have to *know* how something works in order to benefit from the experience. Do you understand all the inner workings of the automobile? I don't and I still drive.

If you are interested in sampling or practicing breath awareness, you can find a suggested plan in the final section of this book.

Meditation

There was a five year period during my corporate career where I traveled eighty percent of the time. During one flight, I remember reading an article about meditation and its benefits. Who wouldn't like to reduce stress, improve their health, increase energy levels, sleep better & achieve a sense of calm? And looking younger, sounded pretty good too. At that moment I thought, "Sign me up. I want all those things!" I think I may have made five attempts before concluding that I wasn't doing it right and abandoned the process. Years later I attended a seminar that included a guided meditation which left me feeling very calm. That's when I knew meditating was going to play a part in the journey into my inside world. I followed through with my commitment to meditate regularly. I practiced enough that the, "I don't know if I'm doing it right," thoughts stopped coming. Today, I really enjoy meditating. Recent thoughts run more along the lines of, "This is so cool!"

There are many different types of meditation. I've used a wide variety of guided meditations designed to lead you through different experiences. A quick search of the internet will provide you with many different options all designed to help make meditating easier. YouTube alone offers hundreds of options.

The best advice I can give you is to avoid overcomplicating the process and keep it simple. There is really nothing for you to do other than observe. Observe your thoughts. Observe your body. Observe what unfolds as you listen to a guided meditation. Observe something of your choice. Observe is not necessarily visual. Listen to a song, focus on hearing every note. There is nothing else for you to do. If you are able to focus your attention, you are doing it right.

At first there will probably be so many thoughts that it's hard to focus on anything. You're likely to get the thought that led me to give up during my first go around, "I'm not doing this right." Please stick with it. If you do, I promise you will benefit physically, mentally and emotionally.

Here's another way to look at it. A main goal of meditating is to *practice* letting thoughts go by. We do this by placing our focus on one thing. Let's say you place your focus on what you see when your eyes are closed. At first, you will probably see nothing but black. But if you keep your focus there you will likely begin to see other things like snow static, colors, morphing shapes, etc. Now, if you don't see anything but black for so many seconds, your mind will start to get bored and impatient. It wants to stay busy, so it will begin feeding you thoughts. A thought may come in like, "What do I need to cover in tomorrow's meeting?" If you follow that thought, you will no longer be focusing on what you see when your eyes are closed. So even if there was anything for you to see, you won't see it. Your mind will have whisked you off to the meeting. However, if you practice bringing your focus back to what you see when your eyes are closed, over time the thoughts will slow. They will still drift in, but it will become easier and easier to let them go by, rather than letting them take you away.

It's like standing at a bus stop. If a bus comes by, you don't have to get on. There will be others coming by like clockwork. Meditating helps us to become more aware of the thoughts coming in and enables us to be more selective of the ones we choose to get on. In other words, you'll begin to read the signs on the front of the bus to know where it's going. "Oh, that one's going to Stress City; I don't feel like going there right now. That one's going to Angrytown. I think I'll wait for the next one to Happyland!"

Your thoughts become options, rather than focus dictators. This skill will then begin to spill over into your everyday life. You'll begin recognizing which thoughts are taking you in a positive direction and those which lead to stress and anxiety. This awareness will help you make conscious choices about where you aim your bow & arrow and thus, how you direct your life.

Awareness of thoughts can also be a great meditation that offers one of my favorite benefits—you begin to hear the quietest personality. This quiet voice is said to be the voice of your higher self. This is the part of you that is completely aware of its connection to all that is. Just like the internet analogy, once connected, you can find anything. That voice knows what's in your best interest. That voice knows the answers to all your questions. You just have to get the personalities of the mind to quiet down enough so you can hear it.

> *"Let us be silent that we may hear*
> *the whispers of the gods."*
> *-Ralph Waldo Emerson (1803-1882)*
> *American Philosopher & Poet*

Think back to the Your Life analogy. When you walk in and meet all the members of your board, know there is one member of that board who knows everything, and I mean everything. He/she is going to be the quiet type, only occasionally vocalizing an idea. Let's call that board member Quiet Voice. His/her ideas may not always make the most sense, especially to the other members of the board. In fact, the rest of the board will be quick and loud with all their logic and reason as to why the suggestion is not feasible and Quiet Voice will not attempt to convince you otherwise. It has no interest in convincing you or attempting to overthrow your free will. But when you are able to find Quiet Voice, you'll know to listen to his suggestions, no matter what the other board members are saying.

Yoga

Over the last few decades, yoga has gradually been embraced in the West. Both men and women are finding amazing physical benefits from practicing yoga. Anyone who thought yoga was more about stretching than strength has been set straight by Madonna's arms!

While most of us in the West are aware of the physical benefits, yoga also offers mental and emotional benefits. Yoga actually means union. Think of it as a union between you and your inside world. A yogi I know explains it as the union of mind, body and soul. By bringing your *focus* to your mind, body and soul, you are really doing a moving meditation.

The initial challenge you can expect with yoga is going to be similar to meditating, the thoughts. Usually in yoga the thoughts seem to be more focused on what your body can and cannot do. Thoughts of how silly you must look, how your poses aren't right or how little you can bend seem to dominate. But you will still be faced with all your other life thoughts, like what you need to do when you're finished, calls you need to make, upcoming appointments, etc. The goal is to keep your focus within, thus uniting the mind, body and soul.

If you are new to yoga, there are many options for you to choose from. There are various types/disciplines of yoga including bikram, power yoga, ashtanga, iyengar and hatha, to name a few. In most cities you will have a variety of yoga studios to select from. Call around and ask questions. Yogi's love to introduce and welcome new people, so let them share whatever hints or insights they may have. Ask them to explain the different kinds of yoga they offer. Ask about any newcomer specials. Many studios will let you sample classes before deciding to enroll in a program, so ask.

Your local hospital may be an option, as well. In Las Vegas, a women's care center that is affiliated with our St. Rose Hospitals offers several different types of yoga, including one for expectant mothers.

If you'd rather practice yoga in the privacy of your own home, there are plenty of videos online.

To ensure you get the maximum benefits from yoga, I would recommend you find an option that moves a little more slowly to begin with. This will help you to really observe how your body feels in each pose. In fact, one of my favorite types of yoga is kundalini yoga. This practice really helps me to focus on synching my breath with my body's movements. I love the following quote from a kundalini yoga set. Please take it with you into any yoga practice you undertake.

"We're not here to prove anything.
We are here to improve everything."
-Guru Singh (Born 1945) Kundalini Yoga Master

With so many flavors of yoga to choose from, keep sampling until you find the one that tastes right to you.

Finding Your Flavors

While I have shared a few of my favorite flavor enhancers, please recognize there are hundreds, if not thousands, of different flavor options for you to choose from. There is a whole industry dedicated to different internal experiences. It's like a never ending buffet. There are different healing modalities focusing on everything from emotional healing (clearing the baggage) to physical healing.

If you are like I was, you are thinking something like, "Just tell me which one works the best, and I'll do that."

This is one area where that philosophy doesn't seem to work. Trust me on this one. I spent a lot of money going in search of the best/most effective one. Lots of people will tell you, "This is the best one." Remember flavor preferences are individual. Just because someone else likes one modality best, doesn't mean you will.

> *"It matters not what road we take but rather*
> *what we become on the journey."*
> *-Michael E. Angier, Founder & CIO of SuccessNet*

A modality's effectiveness seems to be affected by your mindset. That in mind, rather than thinking of the practitioner as one who is going to heal you, I would suggest you enter every experience thinking of yourself as the healer and the practitioner as someone who is there to assist you in your process. Going back to the babysitter analogy, I suggest you don't expect the babysitter to parent your inner child. That's your job.

Sample and create your favorite flavor combos by doing what you in-joy. If there is one place the 60's pop slogan applies, it's in choosing flavors on your journey *in*.

> *"If it feels good, do it."*
> *-Associated perhaps most notably with Woodstock's hippie culture*

Enjoying the Meal on the Go

There are a few things we should discuss candidly before eating this meal on the go or integrating it into your busy life.

Initially, the mind is going to resist this meal. Likely this will happen in one of two ways. The first is going to sound something like, "I know all this." Well, if you do know all this, then I only have one question. How are you benefiting from this knowledge on a daily basis?

> *"Wisdom is meaningless until our*
> *own experience has given it meaning."*
> *-Bergen Evans (1904-1978)*
> *American Rhodes Scholar, Harvard Graduate &*
> *Professor at Northwestern University*

The second response may not even feel like the mind is resisting at all. In fact, the mind will appear to be fully on board and eager to learn more. You may feel like reading the menu just whet your appetite. Please recognize that reading more menus will make you more knowledgeable; but reading will never make you feel *full*. Feeling full is an experience. If you want to feel full, save yourself some time and money and start practicing what you've learned here. *Experiencing is truly the path to ultimate happiness.*

> *"The purpose of life is to live it, to taste your experiences to the*
> *utmost, to reach out eagerly and without fear for*
> *newer and richer experiences."*
> *-Eleanor Roosevelt, First Lady from 1933-1945*

Knowing—Experiencing—Being

I'd like to reinforce this point, since it is common to fall under the misconception that we need to know more. We think we need more knowledge. Our mind *craves* it, convinces us we need it and we can even become addicted to reading menus. We get caught up in reading and learning every concept we come across. The problem is varied terminology can leave us feeling confused. If we are confused, we may not have the confidence to *take* our first bite. If we never take bites and eat this meal, we won't ever get full.

Feeling like we need to know more affects us in many areas of our lives. When was the last time you put off doing something because you just didn't feel like you knew enough?

_____

_____

_____

_____

_____

_____

_____

When I worked in wireless communications, I was always fascinated as I watched the salespeople I would train. Inevitably they would go through a period where they were hesitant to meet with potential customers for fear that they didn't know enough— afraid they wouldn't know *all* the answers to a prospective client's questions. Eventually, they would accept that they may never know everything there was to know about the product they were selling, especially since technology changes almost daily. If they waited until their mind said, "Ok, now we know everything," they may not have ever gotten around to selling anything.

"It's what you learn after you know it all that counts."
-Harry S. Truman (1884-1972)
33rd President of the United States
Also attributed to Hall of Fame Coaching Legend, John Wooden
& Major League Baseball Manager, Earl Weaver

If you are not careful the mind may drive you to become a menu expert. You may know varied terminology with perfect pronunciation and recite teachings at will. If this happens without actually eating the meal and feeding your soul, you will likely get fat with arrogance and superiority; able to see everyone else's issues, but rarely your own. The mind merely attempts to stay in charge. If the mind keeps you busy feeding it, you won't have time to feed the soul.

"To know and not to do is not yet to know."
Zen saying

This very concept is what keeps many people from attaining enlightenment. People get stuck on how much they know. When you know how an enlightened person behaves, you basically have a list of conditions that your mind can now place on you. This list of conditions alone is nothing more than an impossible wish list. The list of conditions will not benefit your soul without the experiential journey *in*.

"There is no more miserable an existence than trying to live like an enlightened person, when one is not enlightened."
-Sri Bhagavan (Born 1949)
Spiritual Leader & Founder of Oneness University

Enlightenment is not about how much you know; it has far more to do with experiencing and being. So, watch out for your craving to know more. Remind yourself that knowing won't satisfy your true hunger.

In the movie Peaceful Warrior, based on the book *Way of the Peaceful Warrior*, Nick Nolte's character says "Knowledge is knowing how to do it, wisdom is doing it."

This is the perfect time for you to begin experiencing. I've told you the inside world holds the answers to all your questions. Rather than ask you to blindly accept that as truth, I will ask that you try it.

"The truth is lived, not taught."
-Herman Hesse (1877-1862)
German Born Swiss Writer, Nobel Prize in Literature (1946)

In other words, don't take my word for it, go straight to the source.

"When you knock, ask to see God—none of the servants."
-Henry David Thoreau (1817-1862)
American Author

This will save you a lot of energy—energy that would be used as the mind would speculate as to the validity of my statements. If you just try it, the mind won't have to spend the energy. You will immediately have first-hand proof through your own experience. Sound like a plan?

Please read the directions for our experiment all the way through before you begin. You may even want to read them more than once. Please make sure you're very clear on what you're going to do before you close your eyes and begin.

In a moment, I'll ask you to close your eyes and begin to focus on your breath. After you've observed a few breaths you'll begin to notice its rhythm. At that point, ask yourself, "Is it true that by *experiencing* the simple things that are outlined in this book, I can open the door to ultimate happiness?" Then wait for an answer.

Sit quietly for at least five minutes and wait for the answer. You may want to use a timer. It can help give you one less thing to think about during the experiment, freeing you to be on the lookout for your answer.

How the answer comes seems to vary by individual. In fact, without the following background, you may not even recognize you were receiving your answer.

For some, answers come in the form of a physical sensation. A yes response may be indicated by goose bumps, a growling stomach or a twitch. You may even feel a pain that'll be gone before you even had a chance to label what it was. It may even feel like an internal energetic sensation like a slow, internal shiver.

Others may receive a visual answer. Colors, shapes or even words may appear from darkness, when your eyes are closed. They may be faint at first or they could just flash for a split second. You may see images that are as clear as photographs. You may not really even see them the way you are used to seeing. It may be more like a feeling that reminds you of a picture in your mind.

You may hear the answer through words or a thought from the quiet voice. If this is your experience, pay careful attention to all the thoughts. How are you going to know which thought is the truth? I would suggest you pay close attention to the urgency of the voice bringing you the thought. Hurried and impatient thoughts are usually from the mind. Again, the quietest, most calm voice is usually a good indicator that it's the one you are looking to hear from. Remember, it has no interest in convincing you or attempting to overthrow your free will. Watch for the negative personalities to chime in right away, telling you the answer is "no" before you've had a chance to see what transpires.

For others the answer may be completely internal, in the form of a knowing, or an intuition. Maybe you've experienced this at some point in your life. Did you ever just know something? You weren't even sure how you knew it, but you just knew it. Your mind had nothing to back it up, but you just knew it. For example, maybe you had a feeling you needed to call someone. When you did, you found your timing was perfect. Maybe you had a bad feeling before someone close to you suffered in some way. Maybe you followed an urge to drive another route home, discovering later you avoided a major traffic delay. Ever wake up knowing "today is going to be a really great day" and it actually turns out better than you could've imagined? These are all examples of how our higher self is aware of, and utilizes, our Oneness.

Regardless of how you get your answer, you will get your answer. But your answers are unique, customized just for you. Some will experience a response immediately. Others may take a few minutes or up to a few days. When I first began to ask questions internally like this, I would usually receive my answer from the outside world within two or three days. Initially, this was helpful to me since I was far more comfortable in the outside world at that time. I would by *chance* pick a book and open to a page that had my answer staring at me in black and white. Sometimes my answer comes in the form of a song or a quote that seems to *randomly* pop into my head.

If you've never tried anything like this before, you likely haven't a clue how your answer will come. This can be a bit of a challenge, but can also be extremely fun. It's a challenge because you have to be open to all directions. Since you don't know where it'll come from, your focus will be shifting in multiple directions. You'll be paying attention to physical sensations, thoughts and in-sights; all while you are careful not to get on the thought buses that can carry you away. After some practice, I quickly found it fun—sort of like my own personal version of "Where's Waldo?"

Please don't stress yourself by worrying that you may miss it. I promise your answer will get your attention. There is one thing that will attempt to distract you in hopes you'll miss it. The mind will attempt to whisk you off on one of those thought buses heading to Worryville, Crazytown or Fearland!

Once you feel comfortable with what you've read, close your eyes and begin to focus on your breath. After you've observed a few breaths you'll begin to notice its rhythm. At that point, ask yourself, "Is it true that by *experiencing* the simple things that are outlined in this book, I can open the door to ultimate happiness?" Then wait for your answer. Ready? Please put the menu down now and begin.

Well, how did it go? Did you feel anything? Did you see or hear something? Did you have any thoughts that offered an answer or insight? Did you notice absolutely nothing? Did you become bored or agitated? Did you feel any discomfort?

"Comfort zones are most often expanded through discomfort."
-Peter McWilliams (1949-2000)
American Self-Help Author

Please make note of what you experienced or what you noticed, if anything, during the exercise.

_____

_____

_____

_____

_____

_____

_____

_____

If you experienced anything at all, notice that your mind automatically wanted to discount it. It may sound something like, "Are you kidding? You think that twitch you had in your left eye was an answer!? Please! That was purely coincidental." Or, "Your stomach growling is not communication from your higher self; it's communication that you're hungry . . . duh!"

Please be aware of the mind's talk. Then commit to trying this once a day for the next seven days. Use the same question. Watch for more *coincidences*. Don't allow the mind to convince you of what the results will be. Complete the experiment and *experience* the results.

While I continue to reinforce the importance of experiencing what you already know, I also accept the mind's desire to learn and know. And I can also tell you, having the mind's buy-in sure helps when navigating the journey *in*. Just like teams in the business world, when everyone's on board, anything can be accomplished. Surely you are aware of some project that may have been unsuccessful because of a few team members' refusal to get on board. Therefore, my recommendation is to indulge the mind's craving to know more just enough to keep it interested and knowledgeable. I suggest that you mentally refer back to the seven courses as you explore other teachings to look for the conceptual similarities, rather than the differences in terminology.

If you find you're reading so much that you don't have time to experience what you've learned, you may get held up. The mind may be trying to distract you. Watch to see if the mind's still running the show. It may be stuck on auto pilot. You may have merely given the mind a new subject to master.

But remember, true mastery lies in 3 areas.

Knowing—Experiencing—Being

"You have to practice becoming alert, becoming more conscious, becoming more aware . . . ."
-Rabbi Irwin Kula (Born 1957)
American Author & President of the
National Jewish Center for Learning & Leadership

I'd like to offer one final suggestion, before I bring you the check. Please re-read our menu often. Your mind may tell you,

"I already know what it says. I just read it." Ask your mind to be open to seeing if it can gain any more knowledge during another read. I promise these seemingly simple menu items offer flavors your palate has yet to explore.

An inmate once said to me, "This book grows. I'm on my sixth time through and I get more every time I read it."

The reality is that this book will help to shift your consciousness. In other words, you grow! So, each time you read it you'll be seeing it from a new perspective. You will receive something new in the inside world every time you read it. Again, I am not asking you to believe me; I am asking you to try it.

Check Please

I began to develop selling skills as a child. Since I started early, I became a successful salesperson. I've closed deals worth millions of dollars. But the ingredients that make up the *7 Course Meal for the Soul* hold far more value than anything I've ever sold. Yet, they are here for the price you paid for this book. The meal may have even been free, if the book was a gift or borrowed. I'm not here to sell you on the book. You've already invested your time reading it.

However, my role as maître d' is far from over. Helping you see that this meal can change your life in ways beyond what you dream possible, is the hardest sale I will ever make. Your mind is going to use everything it's got, in an attempt to distract you from eating. It will tell you it knows enough to keep you happy. If you taste something from our buffet, it will tell you, "Nothing is happening. It's not working." It will tell you this meal takes time that you could be spending on more important things or that the ROI isn't worth it.

I'm not sure it makes me feel better, but I am not alone in my attempt to convince you of the value and power these concepts hold. The quotes I've included span thousands of years. The message is not new. Yet we seem to be more miserable today than at any other time in history. The state of our world shows it. So, if all the greats throughout history have not been able to help us see that our freedom lies in the experience of these ideas, what makes me think I can?

Maybe I'm stubborn or completely crazy, but there's something in me that's compelling me to try. When I told you I really didn't want to write another book on finding happiness, that's the honest truth. If all the greats haven't helped us see how simple it is for us to have the one thing we all truly want, how can I? It seems like a losing proposition. But I've never been good at backing down when I know there's a shot, even if it's a long shot. I tell myself, "even if this book only helps one person, it will be worth it." Now my question is: are you that person?

It is time to present you with the check for this meal, as it does have a price. In fact, this meal has two prices, each requiring different currency.

The first price on your check is paid with *faith*.

You must find faith in the possibilities this meal holds, or at least enough faith to help you take small bites of this meal every day. You need enough faith to quiet the doubts of your mind.

> *"Our doubts are traitors, and make us lose the good*
> *we oft might win by fearing to attempt."*
> *-William Shakespeare (1564-1616)*
> *English Poet & Playwright*

So, exactly how much faith does it take to quiet the doubts of the mind? Your faith must be more persistent than the power and amount of control your mind has had in your life. Meaning, if your mind has been running the show, it is going to throw doubts whenever it feels like you're taking away its power and control.

Faith will not have to sustain you for long though. Because when you eat this meal every day, your experiences will serve as evidence. With every experience, the evidence will mount. After enough evidence, you'll begin to know something is happening. The evidence will prove something is happening. Your mind will eventually accept it as fact. You will begin feeling a freedom you never found in the outside world. Then the need for faith diminishes. After all, how much faith do you need in a proven fact?

Faith is needed when facts have yet to be proven. Faith is required when you believe in things that defy logic and reason. Once you have proof the mind is fully supportive and faith becomes unnecessary.

For you scientifically minded diners, please remember science supports the power of your own intention. If you can find a way to believe in the possibilities, just long enough to get your proof, you might open yourself to even more possibilities.

*"If we were logical, the future would be bleak indeed. But we are
more than logical. We are human beings, and we have
faith and we have hope, and we can work."*
-Jacques Cousteau (1910-1997)
French Explorer & Ecologist

*"Allah is the protector of those who have faith: from the depths of
darkness He will lead them forth into light."*
-Holy Quran, 2:257

The bible says you can move mountains with faith the size of a mustard seed. In this case, to reach ultimate happiness you need enough faith to say, "I will eat this meal for at least seven days, no matter what." Let faith carry you through the week, right past the bus stop of doubts. Taste it each day and the rest will happen naturally. You'll go from tasting, to eating, to savoring it. You'll wonder why you never ate this meal before.

"Some things have to be believed to be seen."
-Ralph Hodgson (1871-1962)
English Poet

The second price on your check is paid with *attention.*

If there is one thing that is required to experience every course in this meal, it's your attention. In the menu, I mentioned the observer role. Each course is experienced by observing something.

observe = pay attention = experience fully

Awareness, observing, focusing on or paying attention to something requires you to be in the present moment. That doesn't mean to think about what's happening. Thinking does not happen in the present moment. If this still doesn't make much sense, please revisit the third course and allow plenty of time for digestion. Just as the mind is bothered when we have faith in something it sees as unproven, the mind is also not very supportive of the second price on your check. When the mind is unsupportive, it will use massive amounts of logic and reason in hopes of proving the prices for this meal are too high.

So, this is it. Here are the 3 objections that make this such a tough sale:

1. Your mind has logic and reason on its side—and I'm asking you to pay the price of having faith, which completely defies logic and reason.
2. Paying attention requires effort and takes time—time the mind could spend on what it believes is more productive like thinking or doing.
3. Your mind has no data to support the effectiveness of passive activities, like observing/paying attention/experiencing.

You will not pay the price for the meal, if the mind convinces you that it's too high. To complete my service, I must address them before you go.

I will do my best to demonstrate to your mind that this price is not only reasonable, but it may actually prove to be a steal. In order to get buy-in from your mind, we must use logic and reason. So, let's talk in terms of return on investment.

In this case, you'd need enough faith to try this for seven days. And let's say you invested twenty minutes a day observing. As with all investments there is a risk. In this investment you are risking two hours and twenty minutes of your time, over the next seven days. You could lose it all. However, if you see even a slight return, you could continue to invest and benefit from compounding. If you look at the forecasted return, which has been projected by wise men and women over thousands of years, it's off the charts. It is projected that you will actually be granted your wish for ultimate happiness. I know, you think those projections are overblown. So, let's say they are. Let's say you got fifty percent happier, would that be worth the investment? What if you were only thirty percent happier?

I can't make the investment decision for you. You see the risk—two hours and twenty minutes. And you understand the potential reward—ultimate happiness. What you do is up to you. To begin with, are you willing to invest two hours and twenty minutes over the first week to see what happens?

In response to the second objection, yes this does take time you could spend doing something else, although it doesn't have to. If you are already busy, the thought of adding another task may sound impossible. But I have some ideas that may help.

I developed a habit of what's popularly referred to as multi-tasking in the corporate world. While most will tell you multi-tasking is not much for helping you stay present, I chose to use this habit to my soul's advantage. I now become aware of my breath during various activities throughout my day. For example, when I'm driving I'll turn off the radio and pay attention to my breathing. And we all have times when someone or something causes us to wait. We wait in lines at the store; we wait for meetings, traffic signals, elevators, kids and appointments. We even wait for tables at other restaurants. While the mind can get bored and agitated if it has to wait, the soul can be nourished during those times if you practice breath awareness or spend the time feeling grateful for all you have. Incorporate gratitude and breath or body awareness during down times you already have in your day and you won't need a lot of additional time in your schedule to turn inward.

> *"Little and often, makes much."*
> *-Anonymous*

What would you have normally been doing in those everyday down times? Maybe thinking or listening to the mind's commentary or judgments. So, you may have to give up a few of those bus rides to Stress City! What else might you miss out on? Normally, you may look for some other suitable activity to occupy the mind. In fact, observe how many times you look at your phone when you have idle time. Since I worked in the wireless industry, I can promise you the phones will hold all important data while you focus on your breath for a few minutes—try it!

If I may, I'd like to speak directly to your mind. So please humor me for a minute.

> Mind,
> I hope you've been listening when I've said what a great and valuable resource you are. I can't even imagine where we'd be without you.
> Your contributions are greatly valued and appreciated. We are finally becoming aware of how much we've actually expected you to do. We've expected you to do everything. We even asked you

to handle the emotions division and we know that isn't even in your scope or area of interest.

While you have gladly taken on all the work, we are beginning to see we have given you too much; too much for anyone to handle. Considering this workload, you've outperformed any expectations we could have had. As a way of thanking you, we'd like to get you some help. We are going to let the body take care of the emotions, so you can be focused on more important things.

Since you'll be more effective when you get sufficient time to rest and rejuvenate, I'd like to propose mini breathing breaks throughout the day.

If these suggestions do not end up being beneficial, we can try something different, or we can always go back to our current method of operation.

Can we count on your support?

During some of these down times where you used to think, you'll still think. This works perfectly as it gives you a great opportunity to observe your thoughts.

Pay attention to all of life and as you take small tastes every day, things will evolve naturally.

"Unless you try to do something beyond what you have already mastered, you will never grow."
-Ralph Waldo Emerson (1803-1882)
American Philosopher & Poet

Please take a moment to review your check. As I mentioned at the beginning of the meal, you will have a choice to pay it, or not. The next and final section offers a payment plan which I think will make it easy, should you choose to pay the price. I trust you will be on your way to a full soul and a life of ultimate happiness, should you choose.

<u>Dining Check</u>

QTY	Menu Item	Price
1	*7 Course Meal for the Soul*	*Faith*
1	*Commitment to pay*	*Attention*

Thank you for dining with us.
We look forward to serving you tomorrow!

You'll find the cashier in your inside world.

Dinner Mint

In lieu of a dinner mint or fortune cookie, I'd like to leave you with a different sweet treat. Please sample some of my other favorite quotes about beliefs, Oneness and self-acceptance.

*"Do just once what others say you can't do, and you will
never pay attention to their limitations again."*
-James R. Cook (1728-1779)
English Explorer

"What a man can conceive and believe, he can achieve."
-Napolean Hill (1883-1970)
American Author of "Think & Grow Rich"

*"One of the greatest discoveries a man makes,
one of his great surprises, is to find he can do what
he was afraid he couldn't do."*
-Henry Ford (1863-1947)
American Founder of Ford Motor Company

*"If we did all the things we are capable of doing,
we would literally astound ourselves."*
-Thomas Alva Edison (1847-1931)
*American Scientist, Businessman & Inventor of the Electric
Light Bulb, Motion Picture Camera & Phonograph*

*"In the province of the mind, what one believes to
be true either is true or becomes true."*
-John Lilly, M.D. (1915-2001)
Physician, Psychoanalyst & Philosopher

*"It's not the events of our lives that shape us,
but our beliefs as to what those events mean."*
-Anthony Robbins (Born 1960)
American Self-Help Author & Motivational Speaker

"Nothing in this world is impossible to a willing heart."
-Abraham Lincoln (1809-1865)
16th President of the United States

"If you think you can, or think you can't, either way, you're right."
-Henry Ford (1863-1947)
American Founder of Ford Motor Company

*"See God in every person, place, and thing,
and all will be well in your world."*
-Louise Hay (Born 1926)
American Author & Founder of Hay House Publishing

"We forfeit three-fourths of ourselves to be like other people."
-Arthur Schopenhauer (1788-1860)
German Philosopher

*"Freedom is not worth having if it does not
include the freedom to make mistakes."*
-Mahatma Gandhi (1869-1948)
Political & Spiritual Leader of India

"It's never too late to be what you might have been."
-George Eliot (1819-1880)
English Novelist

<u>Gratuity or Tip</u>

If you enjoyed your meal and the service you received, rather than leaving a tip, our restaurant's policy is to request that you pay it forward by sharing this meal with others.

The proceeds from this book allow me to continue sharing these concepts throughout the world. Thank you!

Please refer interested parties to our website:

<u>www.7CourseMealfortheSoul.com</u>

Payment Plan

If you have chosen to pay your check, please follow this simple weekly payment plan.

"Success is the sum of small efforts repeated on a daily basis."
-Robert J. Collier (1876-1918)
Publisher of Collier's Weekly Magazine

Morning—8-11 minutes

- While sitting in an alert, upright position, bring your attention to your breath. Take one minute to *feel* grateful.
- For the next five minutes focus on your breath. Don't try to change it. Just keep your focus on how it operates. Get to know how your breath functions. It may help to tell your mind you are going to write a detailed five page report on your breath. Look around the inside world. That's it. Just watch. Pay attention.
- Following your breathing:
  - o 2 mornings—spend five minutes reviewing the first course concepts (once in the beginning of the week, and again 3-4 days later)
  - o 5 mornings—on the other mornings spend two minutes thinking about your inside world and reflect on your experiences there.

Anytime—5 minutes

- Find five total minutes to close your eyes, focus on your breath and explore your inside world. If you need to break it up throughout the day, do it. Just check in whenever you have a minute or more. Look around your inside world, see how it feels. How does it feel to be alive from the inside? Watch how you actually begin to in-joy this as the week progresses.

Before Bed—7 minutes

- Repeat morning breathing—While sitting in an upright position, spend one minute feeling grateful and five minutes focusing on your breath without changing it. Just watch. Pay attention.
- Revisit the experiment—At the conclusion of your breathing, keep your eyes closed and ask yourself "Is it true that by experiencing the simple things in this menu, I can open the door to ultimate happiness?" Then wait for an answer. Sit quietly for at least one minute to see what happens. If you've already received your answer, or you get an answer before the end of the week, ask another question that you would like to have answered.

Initially, changes may be very subtle. You may wish to note any interesting experiences you notice during the week in the journal beginning on page 119. At the end of the week, ask yourself the following questions:

- Did I learn anything?
- Did I feel any emotions?
- Did I feel any physical sensations?
- What changes have I noticed?
- Do I feel different? Would I call that better?
- Has my sleep changed?
- Has my level of energy changed?
- Has the way I deal with stress changed?
- Have other people noticed changes in me?
- How do I feel about the week's return on my investment?
- Is it worth investing another week?

If you choose to continue with this simple payment plan after the first week, you can make the recommended adjustments over the following weeks.

Weeks 2-7

Morning—8-11 minutes

- While sitting in an alert, upright position, bring your attention to your breath. Take one minute to *feel* grateful.
- For the next five minutes focus on your breath. Don't try to change it. Just keep your focus on how it operates. Get to know how your breath functions. Look around the inside world. That's it. Just watch. Pay attention.
- Following your breathing:
  - 2 mornings—spend five minutes reviewing the week's corresponding course of the menu (once in the beginning of the week, and again 3-4 days later)
    - Week 2—2nd Course
    - Week 3—3rd Course
    - Week 4—4th Course
    - Week 5—5th Course
    - Week 6—6th Course
    - Week 7—7th Course
  - 5 mornings—on the other mornings spend two minutes thinking about the week's corresponding course and how you've been experiencing it.

Anytime—5 minutes

- Find five total minutes to close your eyes, focus on your breath and explore your inside world. If you need to break it up throughout the day, do it. Just check in whenever you have a minute or more. Look around your inside world, see how it feels. How does it feel to be alive from the inside? Watch how you actually begin to in-joy this as the week progresses.

Before Bed—7 minutes

- Repeat morning breathing—While sitting in an upright position, spend one minute feeling grateful and five minutes focusing on your breath without changing it. Just watch. Pay attention.
- Personal Question—at the conclusion of your breathing, keep your eyes closed and ask yourself a question of your choice. Although, I would recommend you avoid asking questions about the future. As you experience small miracles in your life,

you will realize you can impact the future. Meaning the future can change. Therefore you may not always get accurate answers to questions about the future. Once you have formulated and asked your question, wait for your answer. Sit quietly for at least one minute to see what happens. If you did not receive an answer in this sitting, watch for your answer to be provided in the outside world as your week unfolds.

At the end of the week, ask yourself the following questions:
- Did I learn anything?
- What did I feel physically? Emotions?
- What changes have I noticed?
- Do I feel different? Would I call that better?
- Has my sleep changed?
- Has my level of energy changed?
- Has the way I deal with stress changed?
- Have other people noticed changes in me?
- Did I enjoy the exercises?
- How do I feel about the week's return on my investment?
- Is it worth investing another week?

Once you have completed seven weeks on this payment plan, I'm certain you've noticed that it has not only become easier, but that you are actually beginning to in-joy it. I encourage you to continue the payment plan, making your own modifications. Feel free to extend your times and begin discovering your favorite flavor enhancers.

Imagine my surprise. After the significant financial investment, time commitment and three trips around the world, I discovered ultimate happiness is found in the inside world. It's a lot closer to home, absolutely free and can be visited each and every day!

Thank you again for allowing me to share this meal with you. Paying this check will reward you in more ways than you can imagine. You'll be glad you didn't dine and dash!

Journal